791.092

KT-234-554

B
F

00007556

NOTHING'S IMPOSSIBLE

Nothing's Impossible

Brian Blessed

LARGE PRINT
Oxford, England

Copyright © Brian Blessed, 1994

First published in Great Britain 1994
by Simon & Schuster Ltd

Published in Large Print 1995 by Isis Publishing Ltd,
7 Centremead, Osney Mead, Oxford OX2 0ES,
by arrangement with Simon & Schuster Ltd

All rights reserved

The moral right of the author has been asserted.

British Library Cataloguing in Publication Data
Blessed, Brian
  Nothing's Impossible. – New ed.
  I. Title
  791.092

ISBN 1-85695-113-8

HEREWARD COLLEGE	
J M L S	02/02/97
	£14.99

Printed and bound by Hartnolls Ltd, Bodmin, Cornwall

This book is dedicated to
Geoff Arkless, a good friend and
a fine mountaineer

CONTENTS

CONTENTS

ACKNOWLEDGEMENTS

Writing this book has proved to be a delightful experience. Rekindling wonderful memories of people, places and events from my adventures and escapades has been all the more enjoyable for giving me the opportunity to work with people I admire and love.

The book has been a team effort and I owe an immense debt of gratitude to John-Paul Davidson, Margaret Magnusson, Adrian Rigelsford, the BBC, the *Daily Mail*, Michael Zimmerman, David Herod, John Haynes and Rachel Bannerman and Electra Georgiadas at De-Winters Publicity for providing me with a fine collection of photographs. I am grateful to Chris Gittins and Roger Lecocq for their research assistance. Heartfelt thanks must go to the staff of the Office of Tibet, London NW6, for all their fascinating information on His Holiness the Dalai Lama.

That splendid actress, Daryl Back, has once again applied her unique skills to the manuscript. With her dedication and keen professional eye, she aided and abetted me until the book was finished.

My P.A., Stephen Gittins, melted my heart with his generous work on every aspect of the book, a minor miracle when you consider he has been managing the ponies and horses and every furry and feathered creature around my home, as well as organising my professional life.

My theatrical agent, Vernon Conway, has broken his back running thither and yon on my behalf, using diplomacy, encouragement and love in dealing with this project. And then, too, there is his charming assistant, Amanda, who has always brought a smile to the proceedings when the rest of us got a bit down.

I am similarly grateful to Simon & Schuster, my admirable new publishers, not least for bringing me into contact with the talented Editorial Director, Martin Fletcher, whom I thank for his subtlety, scholarship and humour.

Whenever I became bogged down and uncertain, my wife Hildegard lent a sympathetic ear and guided me in a new direction. Her great ingenuity and imagination stimulated my mind and got me moving again. Without her inspiration the book would never have been written.

INTRODUCTION

This book is a celebration, an account of some of the adventures in my life. It is not a sequel to my previous biography, *The Dynamite Kid*, nor a precursor to *The Turquoise Mountain*, though in a way it is also a bit of both. We cannot all be Chris Boningtons and Doug Scotts. The adventures I write about can be achieved by anyone with determination and a love of life tempered by a certain amount of healthy madness.

I do hope that there is plenty for everyone's taste. The tales range from exploits with the BBC to mountains, volcanoes, trains, jungles, horses, lamas and giants; even an account entitled "The Ipswich Town Supporter and the Team", which covers one of my favourite adventures, my first musical, *Cats*.

I feel passionately that adventure is immensely important. Now, more than ever, there seems to be a great need for it. Books and films about intrepid explorers have always fired my imagination and left me begging for more. Explorers are our dreams made flesh and blood. Governments spread gloom and doom everywhere and, I think, lack any real vision. Our lives are impoverished by inadequate, limited and unimaginative attitudes, attitudes which send cold shivers through our hearts and insidiously debilitate our aspirations. I will have none of it! To hell with 'em!

My hero, George Leigh Mallory, constantly surfaces

in this book. Writing about mountaineering, he said: "Our case is not unlike that of one who has, for instance, a gift for music. There may be inconvenience and even damage to be sustained in devoting time to music; but the greatest danger is in not devoting enough, for music is this man's adventure . . . to refuse the adventure is to run the risk of drying up like a pea in its shell. Mountaineers, then, take opportunities to climb mountains because they offer adventure necessary to them."

Ladies and gentlemen, we all have our Everests. I wish you happy days. Go for it! And don't let the bastards grind you down.

CHAPTER
ONE

The Statue in the Doughnut

This opening chapter is about a teeny-weeny adventure that I had at BBC Television Centre, Wood Lane, Shepherds Bush, in 1964. The newly appointed Director General was that celebrated senior BBC sage, Huw Weldon. Oh, they were great days, full of imagination, energy and fulfilment. Television Centre was bursting at the seams with high octane talent. The building was six floors high and boasted well equipped studios, workshops, restaurants, tea-bars, offices, wardrobe and make-up departments. It was affectionately nicknamed the Doughnut, as its shape closely resembled that tasty goody.

Looking down from the rarefied atmosphere of the sixth layer of the pastry, Huw Weldon smiled with pride. His tireless commitment to "Aunty Beeb" was everywhere in evidence. At the time I was playing Fancy Smith in the very popular police series, *Z Cars*. This programme had set new standards in live television drama, representing the police in a revolutionary and realistic light, as ordinary people with all the human frailties. The programme starred Joseph Brady and myself in Z-Victor One, James Ellis and Jeremy Kemp in Z-Victor Two, and Stratford Johns, Frank Windsor, Leonard Williams and Terence Edmond located at station headquarters. It was transmitted weekly and each episode lasted fifty minutes. Five minutes were pre-recorded on film, but the remaining forty-five were broadcast live from the studio. It was this vital ingredient that gave the programme its cutting edge. The vulnerability of the artists heightened the quality of the programme. It had a tremendous impact on the public. Sacks full of fan mail arrived daily at the centre, and industrious secretaries painstakingly answered it all.

My character, Fancy Smith, was a rather tough, egotistical, volatile individual, who frequently allowed himself to become emotionally involved with a case. My partner, Jock Weir, played by Joseph Brady, was usually more objective and kept himself at a distance from the social problems we encountered, though he, too, was saddened or moved by the situations we had to deal with. Our characters complemented each other and this balance was also beautifully realised in Z-Victor Two and back at H.Q. between Barlow and Watt.

It was thrilling to be working for the BBC! There I was, part of a corporation that had delighted and enriched my childhood with such radio programmes as *Dick Barton, Paul Temple, Happydrome, ITMA, Much Binding in the Marsh, Henry Hall's Guest Night, In Town Tonight, Rays-A-Laugh, Monday Night at Eight, Band Wagon, Workers' Playtime,* and *Garrison Theatre* with Jack Warner crying out "Mind my bike". If it was music you wanted, in those days you could take your pick from Jack Paynes, Mantovani, Geraldo, Billy Cotton, Charlie Kunz and Forces' Favourites. The BBC also provided us with a feast of classical music, with Henry Wood himself conducting the Proms live from the Albert Hall. Plays poured out of wooden radios, engaged our imaginations and gratified the nation. There was *Saturday Night Theatre* and *Curtain Up*. There were serials to take your breath away. I remember H. G. Wells's *The War of the Worlds* in particular, and Arthur Conan Doyle's *The Lost World*.

To rest and soothe our fevered brains, we could recline by the fireside at night and blissfully fall asleep to "Sailing By", followed by the melodious voice of the BBC announcer giving us the shipping forecast: "Forties, Fisher, Dogger, Humber, German-Bight, Lundy, Fastnet, Irish Sea, Cromerty, Firth, Herigoland! Winds north to north west, fresh to moderate, rising slowly."

As if wanting our last two pennyworth of entertainment, we would awaken briefly from our deep slumber to hear the announcer say: "Goodnight, gentlemen, and good fishing."

Yes, indeed! It was marvellous! We knew we were in good hands with "Aunty Beeb". Whilst we had her Light Programme and World Service we could rest easy and know that God was alive and in his Heaven.

Therefore, you can readily understand how happy I was in 1964, to be part of this fine service. Television Centre felt like my second home. It was a delight to go there. I'd park my black Zephyr Six (the same model as in *Z-Cars*) in the car park, shout a breezy hello to middle-aged, perspiring Vic, the one-armed attendant, throw him my car keys (which he caught like Gordon Banks) and stride towards the front entrance. In reception, the industry of the place would hit me. It was like being in a beehive: frenzied, yet orderly. Casts of many different shows jostled to get the keys to their dressing rooms, and artists dressed and ready in their costumes waited to board the buses that were to take them to nearby locations.

The curving corridors of the Doughnut housed numerous dressing rooms and wardrobe and make-up facilities. The pride and joy of the building were the two main large studios, named "Red" and "Blue Assembly". Work had started on a new studio called "Green Assembly", which would bring much needed relief to the overworked blue and red ones. These studios operated a kind of rota system and housed programmes such as *Dixon of Dock Green, Compact, Doctor Who, Z-Cars, Top of the Pops, Val Doonican, The Benny Hill Show, Steptoe and Son, Hugh and I, Doctor Finlay's Casebook, Maigret, Juke Box Jury, Mogul, Not Only but Also, Sykes, The Ken Dodd Show, The Newcomers, Comedy Playhouse, Play of the Month, Play of the Week, The Wednesday Play, The Sunday Play*, and of course Michael Bentine's *Square World*.

If there was any danger of silence, this was quickly rectified by the cast of *Square World*. This marvellous original programme, the forerunner of Monty Python, opened up new frontiers. It was not unusual to see German SS Soldiers from this show goose-stepping through reception and spilling on to the forecourt, not to mention the occasional Red Indian.

Not unlike Barrie's play *Dear Octopus*, the BBC stretched its loving tentacles far and wide; there were studios at Lime Grove and of course, that other temple of excellence, Broadcasting House. Within Television Centre, programme planners, producers, directors and staff were in hot pursuit of "the very best". Shaun Sutton, in particular, was an inspiration to us all. He was often seen on location directing two camera teams at the same time. It was no sweat to him and he revelled in the challenge. Yes! That's the word. Challenge! Everybody took it up like an Olympic torch and passed it on to the next competitor.

Often, in spite of the fine ventilation in the studio, I would seek opportunities during rehearsals to get a breath of fresh air in the inner courtyard of the Doughnut. There you could sit on a wall that surrounded a small raised circular patch of grass and catch the afternoon sun. I was always surprised that, although the building towered on all sides, the sun seemed to pour its rays into this little sanctuary. In the middle of the grass circle was an elegant fountain, which was lit up at night and glistened magically. Jets of water rose into the air and fell back into a large stone saucer about fifteen feet in circumference. In the centre was a tall concrete column over twenty feet high, rather like Cleopatra's Needle. On the top of this was a bronze statue of Helios, the all-seeing sun god of Greek mythology. So, I suppose it was perfectly understandable that the little courtyard always caught the sun.

I used to enjoy shouting up to Huw Weldon's offices on the sixth floor. There he would sometimes hear me and would throw open the windows and respond good-naturedly to my banter. It was common to see him motoring around the studios offering words of advice and encouragement, praising unreservedly any work that satisfied his high standards.

You may feel that I carry too bright a torch for the splendid Director General, but, during my short acquaintance with the gentleman, he left a deep and lasting impression on me. His visits to the studios were eagerly awaited and left everyone feeling that they were part of The Team. The electricians and camera crews called him "The Guv", an expression that amused him enormously and indicated how easily they could relate to him. He was always accessible and sympathetic to anyone's problems, and he had a tremendous sense of humour.

I remember sitting in the waitress service area of the canteen with him one day, as he pinned my ears back about my performance in *Z-Cars*. "Great heavens, Blessed! You were awfully tough last night! I think you're getting a little too aggressive. Not that the public mind, they seem to love it. Still it may be wise to exercise a little restraint. Then again, I may be absolutely wrong! I frequently am! So, dear boy, you may want to take what I have said to heart or completely ignore it!" He wheezed with laughter and got stuck into his salad.

"How can I ignore you, Huw?" I replied. "I understand from certain high-ranking officials here that you are 'He Who Must Be Obeyed'!"

He chortled merrily and retaliated: "'He Who Must Be Obeyed'? Really, Blessed? That can't be true, you're having me on. It suggests that I know what I'm talking about and I leave that distinction to fellows like you!"

I continued: "Obviously you do suffer from knowing what you are talking about for you are also called 'The Wise Owl'."

"As always, Blessed, you are talking utter unmitigated tommy rot! I suggest you give up acting and take up the diplomatic service! By the way, how do I look? I've been up half the night entertaining royalty! God! I thought that they would never go home. In the end I was so fed up, I walked into the room where they were still drinking and said, 'Haven't you people got any palaces to go to?!' That did the trick and they all buzzed off, as I must now. So please excuse me, I have a documentary to view. Oh! Dear fellow! I do miss directing and editing. I used to find it so restful, rather like a waltz, one-two-three — cut! one-two-three — cut! Simple, so simple. Cheerio, dear boy."

Some weeks later, I was in a cricket match with him on the sixth floor. The bat we were using was of the very best, having been autographed by Len Hutton himself, but the rest of our equipment was very dubious to say the least. The wicket was a dustbin and our ball had strayed from the tennis court. Still, we were enjoying ourselves. The players were actors, producers, directors and anybody who felt that way inclined. Norman Rutherford proved to have a good googly and Elwyn Jones, our boss on *Z-Cars*, was a useful bat, as was the Director General. Huw drew me aside and told me that his mother had come to visit him and was busy tucking into some sandwiches in a room close by.

"I wish you would help me out with a ticklish problem," he whispered conspiratorially. "You see, Blessed, my mother thinks I don't like *Doctor Who* and am planning to axe the programme — which is absolute nonsense! She positively loves the good doctor and is particularly enamoured of the Daleks. Would you mind popping in and having a word with her to reassure her! She will be absolutely thrilled, as she is a big fan of *Z-Cars*. Perhaps she will believe you, as she refuses to believe me!"

"Of course, Huw," I replied, and made my way down the corridor.

After gaining admittance and introducing myself, I found Mrs Weldon, as Huw had said, tucking into a sandwich and enjoying a cup of tea. She was a lady in her late sixties or early seventies and she enquired how I was and offered me a cake. Readily accepting this, I carefully and subtly explained that I, too, loved *Doctor Who* and that it was inconceivable that it would be taken off the air.

Mrs Weldon smiled, thanked me and said how much she enjoyed *Z-Cars*. After a slight pause she added, "But I don't like you, I like the Scotsman!"

She was of course referring to my mate Jock in Z-Victor One. I smiled and thanked her for her kindness and bade her good-day, offering her a hidden "V" sign as I closed the door.

In 1965, I purchased a house in Richmond, Surrey

called Clarence House. It had quite a history and had belonged to William the Fourth. Apparently it had been his summer residence. It was rumoured that he had lived there with the famous actress Mrs Jordon, then it became the John Butt School and thereafter had gradually been allowed to become run down, which was a great shame.

The work it took to restore it went on for months and months, dust and filth everywhere. One day, I drifted up Richmond Hill in a dream-like state to get away from the chaos. I was hailed from a doorway by an austere gentleman, with a fine, modulated voice.

"What on earth are you doing, you dreadful young man! I saw you on ITV the other day, absolutely disgraceful! Have you no principles?"

It was of course, none other than Huw Weldon! His grin broadened, as his colourful voice echoed around the Georgian facades. "You must only work for the BBC, anything else is unacceptable. It is tantamount to treachery. However, on this occasion, I will, considering your previous record, grant you a reprieve and invite you in for a coffee."

Sharing half an hour with Huw in his home was a privilege. Free from the demands of Television Centre and with the phone off the hook, he relaxed and waxed lyrical about all he loved and believed in. With grace, wit and vision he expressed his boundless love for the British Broadcasting Corporation.

"We're seventy thousand strong, Blessed! All active and expanding! Though not too far or too fast. No country has anything to compare with us, except possibly Japan. Yes, there's a certain company there, that is a little like us. Why do I think it so important, eh Blessed? Because the BBC is the heart and soul of Britain, reaching out and touching everyone. To the rest of the world, the Corporation conveys in numerous ways the spirit of these islands. And what is that? Throughout our history Britain has produced poets, painters, writers, actors, singers, dancers . . . the whole kingdom for hundreds of years has produced art on a vast scale. Why, Blessed? The answer is quite simple. It is a mystery!"

I left Huw's house that day deeply moved, newly aware that the BBC had influenced my life from the day I was born.

Now that I have introduced you to the man as I knew and loved him, I return to 1964 and the adventure I promised you in the first sentence of this chapter; an adventure in which Huw was the chief protagonist.

It was after midnight on a dark winter night at Television Centre and no one was about. Security in those days was easy going and relaxed. Only one young lady occupied the desk in reception, and the attendant at the front gate was happy and sleepy. All the programmes had long been put to bed for that day and the studios were dark. All was quiet. Huw Weldon and I, carrying a long aluminium ladder, tip-toed towards the inner courtyard of the Doughnut and the fountain in the middle.

I might add in passing that we had indulged beforehand in a little refreshment in his office! Suffice it to say, we were as pissed as newts. We spoke in whispers.

"Follow me silently, not a movement heard must be, here's the place, mask yer face, have yer ladder handy!"

"Follow me, Blessed," muttered Huw. "Don't worry, no one can see us, I've had Vic turn off the fountain so you won't get wet!"

"Are you sure you want to do this, Huw?" I enquired. "Anyway, I might not be able to shin up it."

"Nonsense," Huw scoffed. "You'll get up easily. You're Fancy Smith aren't you?" He grinned.

I must explain that Huw was very proud of the statue of Helios the sun god and he passionately felt that it was neither observed nor appreciated by anyone. Therefore, he wished to bring close attention to it by having me perform a certain deed.

Huw's dark-brown eyes were full of mischief as he laid the ladder against the concrete saucer of the fountain. He held it firmly, as I commenced to climb slowly into the circular saucer. God knows why no one saw us, maybe they were looking the other way. The whole escapade reminded me of the dares I used to do as a child, in Yorkshire. We called them "dasties".

Now came the tricky part of the operation: shinning up the concrete column. All went well for a few feet, but then I slithered down again. My shoes didn't help, so I took them off. This did the trick and gradually I gained height and finally arrived at the statue.

"Well done, Blessed!" whispered Huw. "Now tie it on." With that order from "He Who Must Be Obeyed", I took out a "french-letter" (condom) and started to blow it up into a balloon. When it was a good size, I tied a knot in it and with great difficulty taped it to the penis of Helios!

"Jolly good," said Huw. After a pause he added, "Now I hope people will take notice of the bloody thing!"

I would like to add, with apologies to the Sun God, that a certain receptionist at Television Centre has informed me that Helios is known affectionately as "Golden Bollocks". So it would appear that Huw got his wish after all.

In Memory of Huw Weldon. 1916–1986.

CHAPTER
TWO

Incident at Innsbruck and Adam and Eve

In 1969, I was offered my first part in a film, *The Last Valley*, written and directed by James Clavell, the author of *Shogun*. The film starred Michael Caine and Omar Shariff and was to be shot on location in and around Innsbruck, Austria. It depicted events during the Thirty Years War in the 1600s, and I was to play Korski. Korski only appeared at the beginning, but Clavell assured me that it was a most effective part with a glorious death!

"I promise you," he said with conviction. "There is nothing like a good death to start your film career!"

I was an out and out baddie, who exploded onto the screen and killed everyone in sight, including an old peasant, played by a respected character actor, Martin Miller. Martin was eighty years old at the time and during the car journey from the Marie Therese Hotel in Innsbruck to the high snow-covered valleys in the mountains, he expressed to me his concern about going to altitude at his age. The location that day was at 8,000 feet and he had very mixed feelings about it.

As the car climbed ever higher, the old man's face became ashen and I urged him to go down again.

"To hell with the film, Martin! It's not worth risking your life! I'll ask the driver to turn round and take you back."

But he said that if he did, the rot would set in. He would start making all kinds of excuses for not accepting work anymore and end up never going beyond his garden gate. My pleas, therefore, fell on deaf ears and we arrived at the new altitude and changed into our period clothes.

An hour or so later I charged down the slope on a black horse, wielding a black, papier mâché mace and pretended to strike Martin down. It was a long shot — the actual blow, of course, was to be received by a padded, stunt man.

My job was to miss the old boy by about a yard, at which moment he would fall down, to assist the edit to the stunt man. However, Martin fell down far too early, when I was still some twenty yards away. I reined in my horse and pulled his leg about his dreadful timing. There was no response. On closer examination we discovered that tragically he had died of a heart attack. The rest of the day's filming was abandoned.

Later, I sat in my tent and drank coffee. The whole scene was horribly depressing. "Mountains! You can stuff 'em," I thought. The death of that sweet man in that desolate terrain distressed everyone and the dangers of the altitude were suddenly appreciated. The actors and film crew had been playing football matches at lunchtime — at between 8,000 and 9,000 feet! We played with speed and fury, our hearts beating ten to the dozen and our lungs heaving fit to burst, only pausing when we felt nausea or giddiness approaching. What fools! What ignorance!

However, as time passed, I settled down again and enjoyed my surroundings. My part, though small, took weeks to film, as the character appeared in several different locations. This afforded me the opportunity to travel extensively through Austria. The rich variety of that splendid country with its intriguing history and architecture, its numerous concert and opera houses, gave me great pleasure.

In the Marie Therese Hotel, I occasionally shared a relaxing coffee with Omar Shariff and listened to his stories of his homeland, Egypt. As he is on screen, romantic and mysterious, so he is in life, revealing a fine appreciation of women and bridge and a gentle sense of humour.

"I enjoy everything in this country, Brian," he said, "except its damn mountains. I positively hate them. The altitude makes me sick, I have been vomiting all morning — a daily ritual up here — and it is taking all the fun out of making the film!"

Poor Omar! Two days before I had seen him get out of his car, curse the mountains and hold his stomach, as he contorted in agony.

Though I was spared altitude sickness and the rampant "Innsbruck Trots" that had decimated most of the cast and crew, my appreciation of the Austrian mountains did not exceed Omar's to any great degree. Without doubt the rich green valleys, with their meandering rivers, picturesque meadows and towering trees reaching up to the mountains, pleased the eye and relaxed the heart and mind. But, somehow, the picture was too perfect: predictable and uniform.

Making *The Last Valley* was a happy experience for everyone involved. The director and his management were inordinately kind to us, doing everything in their power to make us comfortable. The cast was large, including sixty to seventy actors and scores of excellent stunt artists. The only sour note was that the Marie Therese Hotel was taking us to the cleaners!

With such a large cast it was imperative, for the first few weeks, that we stay together for transport convenience. As we were playing mercenary soldiers from the Thirty Years War, we looked a pretty fierce bunch — Yours Truly looking the worst.

My costume was black leather with silver spiked studs, which had once been worn by that brooding star, Jack Palance, when he played Attila the Hun. With my rather large arms, cropped hair, short beard and weapon (the aforementioned large black mace), I looked exceedingly fearful.

Austrians, who came to watch the filming, would point to me on my black horse, called The Devil, and say, "Look at zat one! What a brute!"

The people of Innsbruck generally found our appearance very intimidating and, although we behaved impeccably, they reacted to us nervously. When I walked down the street I felt like some dangerous barbarian. My kindly, casual "Good evening's" or "Hello's" caused mayhem, as mothers and fathers pulled their teenage daughters into side streets or shop doorways to avoid me.

16

The restaurant, the Golden Addler, was the one place I felt accepted and at home. It was frequented by the local and visiting opera companies and the soft warm lights and candles made my spirits rise. The music cheered me and set my feet tapping.

The star of this jolly place was a huge lady of twenty stone or more, by the name of Friedel. She played the accordion with great skill and she possessed a rather sweet, honeyed voice. There is no doubt that this gigantic lady found me most appealing. On our first encounter, she threw her accordion aside, enfolded me in her massive arms and exclaimed, "Oh, my lovely Rasputin!"

When she discovered I could sing, the world was my oyster. I was constantly requested to render "When Irish Eyes Are Smiling", and my rendition of "Danny Boy" was guaranteed to bring the house down. There were benefits as a result — free meals whenever I liked — so, I suppose, I sang for my supper! These perks also embraced my circle of friends and we enjoyed many colourful evenings of free-flowing, bubbling, warm wine, interlaced with melody and dance. Tenors, baritones, basses and sopranos from the opera filled the room with glorious sound, heady stuff and great fun.

One evening Michael Caine, watching it all, commented with a wry smile, "I must say, Brian, you don't half have a way with the birds!"

Michael is renowned, not only for his marvellous acting, but also for his stories and he regaled us with quite a few. In *The Last Valley* he played the leading role of the Captain. From what I can gather, it is a performance of which he has always been particularly proud. I have always been a fan of his, and I agree with him that it is one of his very best performances.

Throughout all the fun and games at the Golden Addler, things were warming up in quite a different way at the Marie Therese Hotel. A new influx of stunt artists, needed for the large battle scenes, had swelled the ranks of the British. In tune with everyone else, they were experiencing over-enthusiastic bills from our hosts.

The bubble finally burst one evening in the posh hall with the cabaret and dancing areas. Austrian men took offence at the barbarians dating their willing Brunhildas, and tempers started to rise.

All in all, numbers were fairly evenly matched, but the British contingent sported several retired heavyweight boxers and highly trained karate experts. I viewed it all with some amusement from a small table near the exit door, at the same time reading my esoteric and engrossing book, *The Bhagavad Gita*, which was resting against a bowl of flowers.

Except for an occasional movement to avoid some flying missile, I remained perfectly still in the true British manner and continued to enjoy my meal. The battle took on epic proportions, as chairs, tables and bodies flew in all directions.

Two of the most colourful stunt artists in the business, ex-heavyweight boxer Nosher Powell and his cruiserweight champion brother, Dinny, politely enquired if I would mind holding the glass doors open, to assist them in disposing of the Hun bodies. It was the least I could do, as it in no way interfered with my eating! In fact, one diligent waiter even managed to bring me my pudding! My only other duty was to ensure that all ejected Huns remained outside. To this end, if any poked their dazed heads back through the door, I impressed upon them the error of their ways with a hefty round-house punch to the chops.

The conflict was reasonably short and the "Dam Busters" march would have been most appropriate, as the triumphant winners were without doubt the Brits. The hotel, surprisingly, took it all in its stride and no complaints were made, a further indication that the cost of the damages had been more than covered by the profits from the British clientele.

The next day, having spent several hours soaking my hands in iced water to reduce the swelling, I decided to go for a walk. The afternoon was quiet and peaceful, with the warm rays of the sun piercing the fleeting clouds.

All in all, I felt curiously happy. My journey took me past small houses straight out of *Grimm's Fairy Tales*, over hump-backed bridges and, finally, to a point at the bottom of the valley. Resting there, I took in my surroundings.

A single road wound up the hillside and disappeared into the distance among the dense tall trees. The sun continued to shine and I found myself meandering up this road and gaining height slowly. After only a few minutes of ascent, the view changed. I noticed the different colours and shapes of the rooftops and church spires. At the outset they had towered above me; now they were level with my eyeline.

My body eased imperceptibly into a gentle rhythm, a feeling almost like floating. A sensation of happiness grew and my movement flowed in harmony with my breathing. My mind and being embraced the widening horizon. Going uphill was irresistible and all prosaic hopes and fears melted away.

On, on, on. Yard after yard. My breathing was soft and deep. Each new corner, as I rounded it, presented a new surprise. The trees, ruffled by the wind, revealed their inhabitants to me: the birds and the butterflies.

Moving ever upwards, a feeling of grace enveloped me, the like of which I had never experienced before. Time stood still as I paused, not moving a muscle. All was one. The world and I were indivisible.

How long I stood on the road like this, I cannot tell. I became aware of the sun's rays across the trees and then, with almost unbearable beauty, the sound of the church bells sailed up the valley and reverberated in my head. Masses and masses of church bells singing their individual songs.

In my present state, so alive to my surroundings, the bells released my emotions and, quite unable to control myself, I started to shake, tears poured down my face and I felt as though cascading waterfalls had burst from my mind and had plunged down my spine.

Apart from childhood, I had never cried and I was utterly confounded. "The mountains!" I whispered. "The mountains! Why on earth have I missed them before?"

Standing as I was at about 5,000 feet, the range of these giants loomed over me. There they were, bearing such names as Brandjoch, Sattelspitzen, Reither Spitze,

Kleiner Solstein, and the higher Zugspitze. Scores of peaks, as far as the eye could see. Why had I never appreciated their awesome beauty before? Long forgotten words by George Leigh Mallory burned in my head: "It was as if I was penetrating a secret."

I had a searing urge to get to the top of the nearest peak. I raced up the road and through the trees at a rate of knots and found myself labouring for breath at the foot of the scree slopes below a mountain named Hafelekar.

I was ignorant of the fact that a considerable amount of time had elapsed and, despite the setting sun, I made my way up the torturous scree, gaining two feet and sliding down again, losing one in the process. It was getting really late when I finally arrived at the base of the rock face, from where I could see numerous routes to the summit, all seductively inviting. There, in spite of my brand new passion for the mountains, good sense prevailed and I made my way down.

It was almost dark and Innsbruck's evening lights seemed far away. The story of my descent is best left untold. Suffice it to say, that when I limped into the hotel, my legs were a mess and my feet blistered.

But from that day I was hooked. My desire to climb was insatiable. Taking advice from the climbing shops in the area, I purchased a fine pair of boots, studied maps and routes and ascended beloved Hafelekar and the other peaks. I almost became the wild man of the mountains; everything else took second place. The second assistant on the film had hell locating me; he had to send runners up the mountains to look for me.

"Come on Brian," would be the cry. "We bloody need you for filming!"

At night, I found it impossible to still my thoughts. Images of gullies, ridges and chimneys pervaded my dreams.

Some of the actors asked if they could come with me, intrigued by my obsession. On one such trip I was accompanied by that fine artist, Nigel Davenport. Walking gently towards Seegrube, a thousand feet below Hafelekar, Nigel said, quite rightly, that he felt he had walked far enough. Bearing in mind that this was his first trek, he had done very well.

Puffing my chest with pride and assuming the air of a Chris Bonington, I opened my small rucksack and poured him a coffee from my Thermos, plus the customary Mars Bar. This ensured that my companion had plenty of sustenance for the return journey. Nigel was duly impressed by my solicitude and murmured, "I feel I'm in good hands. You're obviously very experienced."

I smiled modestly and deceitfully but, what the hell, I was enjoying myself.

We relaxed in the lovely pastoral setting and chewed the fat comfortably together, Nigel expounding splendidly on the meaning of life. Eventually we returned to the topic of mountains.

"Hell, Brian!" he confessed. "I no longer have the fitness for this kind of caper. You should see my brother, he's fantastic! Owns a dairy farm; works night and day and hasn't an ounce of fat on him. His body is lean and wiry, with amazing stomach muscles. I suppose that's the kind of fitness you would need to climb Everest!"

This sudden mention of Everest took me by surprise, for I had not thought about it for years.

"Everest?" I stuttered.

"Well," continued my companion, "that monolith makes these mountains look a bit sick! Getting up that awful South Col was a huge problem. By God, that must have been bloody tough! It's not a place I'd care to be. I take my hat off to that expedition of 1953."

His words had an immediate effect, unlocking doors in my mind that had been long closed. Back at the hotel, I lay on the bed and stared at the ceiling. Everest. I remembered the book about Mallory I had borrowed as a child from a friend and never returned. I remembered my Dad's stories about the 1920s expeditions and the mystery of the disappearance way up there of Mallory and Irvine in 1924.

An hour or so passed and the phone rang several times, as various actors enquired when I was coming down to dinner. Eventually I let it ring and ring.

It was all so tantalising! What was Everest? Why Everest? Where exactly was it? The highest place on Earth!

In the end, I pulled myself together and went to dinner.

Of course, over the weeks, the more I attempted to push it out of my mind, the more the great mountain dominated my thoughts.

At the time, I was going out with a splendid young lady by the name of Ilona Rodgers. Ilona had blonde hair, blue eyes and was as pretty as a picture. She was a fine actress and had appeared in numerous films and tellies. She was a wonderful friend and confidante.

Back in London, in her apartment, I would ramble on for hours and hours about the world's highest mountain. Although she was always understanding and sympathetic, she also found me ridiculously funny.

I told her I intended to climb Everest one day. As my emotions grew in intensity, so did her mirth. She lost control completely and roared with laughter. This was exactly what I needed, as I was becoming a terrible bore. It was all well and good to have grandiose ideas, but in reality, my ability as a climber extended only to a possible attempt at Boxhill in Dorking!

With tears of laughter still on her face, Ilona stroked my hair and said, "Darling Brian, let me see what books I can find on the subject. In the meantime, I suggest you try and book yourself on a climbing course in Wales."

Ilona was marvellously disciplined and brilliant at organising things. She quickly spread an array of climbing magazines in front of me, underlining several climbing clubs, that might be of help. After a great deal of deliberation over several mugs of coffee, the name Geoff Arkless caught my eye.

"I like the sound of that," I said. "Geoff and Breda Arkless of Deiniolen in North Wales. Arkless! It brings images to the mind of a large, weather-beaten Titan of the Mountains."

A few weeks later, driving my old Z-car, I arrived in Llanberis one wet afternoon, ready to begin my one-week course. The streets were almost deserted and I was beginning to feel lonely and out of place, when a small van drew up and a petite man of medium height got out and addressed me. It was Mr Arkless.

His appearance bore no resemblance to my expectations. Blowing on his hands and rubbing them rhythmically to keep out the cold, he reminded me somewhat of a mountain goat. The impression was further enhanced by the fact that he sported a short, thin Nanny-goat beard. The biggest surprise of all was that he spoke in a high-pitched voice with a Geordie accent.

"Hello, Mr Blessed. Welcome to Llanberis. You've arrived on a wet and windy day! I do hope that you had a pleasant journey?"

I replied in the affirmative. He continued, "I hope you don't mind but, of course, I do recognise you."

"Not at all," I replied. "I'm delighted. Call me Brian."

He smiled at this. "Ah, the price of fame, Brian . . . the price of fame. My name's Geoff. I'll show you to your guest house and then I'll explain what the week's itinerary is going to be."

He was kind, meticulous, and punctual. I had purchased my climbing boots at the YHA in Southampton Street in London and the staff there had informed me that Geoff was one of the safest climbers in the country and that I couldn't be in better hands. Nevertheless, I still could not conceive of him holding me should I fall off any cliff. I was about fifteen stone and was about twice his size!

"You look fit," he said the next day. "But you're heavily muscled."

"I've done a lot of judo."

"Well, young Mr Blessed, Sir, let's see how you make out at climbing."

My "making out" proved pretty poor, as I struggled with my first lesson in absailing.

"Relax, Brian. Take it steady — there is no rush," my teacher gently advised.

I remained uncoordinated and stiff and, during my first experience on a small rock face, I felt nothing but sheer, blind panic. My clumsy attempts to find the foot holds were pathetic and I felt a complete bloody fool. Throughout this, I could hear Geoff's sharp instructions biting into my head: "Keep yer heels down, use yer eyes! Try and keep yer body away from the rock face. Oops! I'll try and pretend that I didn't see that! Yer not supposed to use yer knees. Have patience, it will become second nature in time. After all, I'm sure I would look just as silly if I tried to perform in front of a camera!"

It was all double dutch to me and I yearned for the day to end. But the following day, I experienced the same fear, as Geoff took me up a variety of routes. Only one day did I enjoy myself. Geoff informed me that on completing a climb of Tryfan, I would meet a couple of friends at the top. On reaching the summit, Geoff pointed to the two personalities — a pair of rocks!

"They're known as Adam and Eve, Brian. Say hello."

It was a sweet moment and it eased my tension. Nevertheless, I approached each morning with new dread and prayed for the time to pass quickly so that I could return to the peace of my bed.

The highlight of the trip was undoubtedly a visit to Geoff's home to meet Breda, his wife and their six children. Their warmth and hospitality made it an evening to savour.

The last day was to be an ascent of Snowdon, by the Crib Goch Ridge. The wind blew hard and it rained heavily. Certainly, I was honoured to climb the famous mountain for the first time in my life but I shook with fear when we approached any section that was even mildly exposed.

It took all my acting ability to convince my tutor that I was having a wonderful time, underplaying, rather than overplaying, my part. I wonder if he was convinced?

On arriving back in London, Ilona couldn't wait to hear the news. Had it worked out well? Had it fulfilled my expectations? A huge pot of tea was laid out in front of me and a mighty, colourful salad, containing all kinds of goodies.

"Well? Well? Well?" she questioned. "Tell me. Go on tell me! I'm dying to hear!"

Fortunately, she gave me no time to reply and continued, "Look, look what I've found. All the Everest books of the 1920s. They're all wonderful and in pristine condition. But do tell me, please. I'll bet it was wonderful!"

Her kindness and enthusiasm made things much worse. I could bear it no longer.

"Quiet, Ilona! For God's sake, shut up! You have to understand that the whole thing was dreadful!

"I'm sorry to have to disappoint you, please forgive me, but I hated it from start to finish. I feel positively ashamed! Most of the time I was consumed with fear and couldn't cope remotely. That's a new experience for me. I thought that I could face anything. Jesus Christ! I never, as long as I live, ever want to go near a mountain again. Never, bloody ever! Do you hear me? Just feel my damp shirt underneath my jersey. That's not sweat from hard labour, that's perspiration from cold bloody fear — fear of Snowdon today. Horrible! Horrible!

"Geoff Arkless is sweet, nice, lovely, but he wasted his time with me. The worst was when I followed him on the Flying Buttress! This was my first climb and classed as only 'difficult'. Climbers don't even rate it! I was absolutely paralysed with terror. Not fear, woman — terror!

"It started to rain and the water poured down the rocks and into my face. My boots slipped and I grabbed the rope in desperation. I couldn't see a thing. My fingers were numb and they bled, as I tore my nails trying to find hand holds. And Geoff's voice kept whining through it all: 'Keep yer heels down, Brian. Use yer eyes.' 'What bloody eyes?' I shouted back.

"To top it all, climbing the ridge to Snowdon, I peered down the so-called beloved black rock face, Cloggy. God in Heaven! What a shocking precipice. Do you know, there was a small boy climbing it with others of a similar age. They couldn't have been more than fourteen. There they were, as relaxed as you like, and there I was on an easy scramble shaking like a baby. Later I saw the same boy waiting for a bus — he was so young, he should have been in bed hours ago.

"No, Ilona. It's over. I tried but I was gutless. My experience in Innsbruck was just stupid and romantic!"

"Oh no, Brian," she said. "That's not true."

"Look, Ilona. The night I visited Geoff at his home, I met a young professional climber, who a few months previously had fallen during a new climb on Cloggy. You should have seen his arms, legs and shoulders — his so-called 'healed scars'. They looked like red raw meat, as if he'd been half-devoured by some monster from a horror film."

The outburst was over. I pitched myself on to the sofa and was silent.

My catatonic, self-pitying state was interrupted by a large mug of tea, which was placed carefully in my hands. During the first few sips my friend whispered in my ear, "Oh, Sir Brian, as bold as a lion. Now you're not so bold anymore!"

She was reciting a poem she remembered from her childhood. Ilona always recited this verse to me.

"I'm looking at a sad toad, a depressed toad, indeed, a smelly toad, who needs a bath!" she continued, referring of course to Kenneth Grahame's *Toad of Toad Hall*.

I smiled and felt daft. Ilona had a gift for making me laugh at myself. Within five minutes I was tucking into the salad and enquiring what was on at the local cinema.

After the highly recommended bath, I gingerly fingered the Everest books, affecting only a mild interest in them. They were the three volumes covering the 1921, 1922, and the tragic 1924 British expeditions; the latter being the one I had read as a child. I flicked it open with studied indifference, for the benefit of the resident spy in the kitchen, who said ever so quietly, "A curious toad!"

Pandora could not have been so bewitched as I. Oh

29

yes indeed! Hour upon hour, with constant supplies of tea, I was engrossed in those fabulous books.

At three o'clock in the morning I finally lay back on the sofa to digest the exploits of those wonderful men. What courage, what tenacity and what vision! Their names were so haunting and yet so terribly British: Bullock, Somerville, Norton, Younghusband, Longstaff, Bentley, Beetham, Odell, Noel, Moorshead, Howard-Bury, Kellas, Wheeler, Heron, Wollaston, Bruce, Hazard, Irvine. And the Bayard of the mountain himself — George Leigh Mallory.

Sleep that morning was hard to come by, as I dreamt of men and mountains. The books overcame the traumas of Snowdon. Now I was Toad again: the Traffic Queller of the highways, the Mighty Conqueror, the Intrepid Mountaineer!

It would be a gross exaggeration to say that my trip to Wales had changed me, but there was a difference, a definite difference. The rugged landscape and my struggles in its dark mountains had kindled a stubbornness and a will to "do well" that has grown over the years.

During the following months a steady stream of activities took me far and wide in pursuit of the noble sport, always with the loyal Ilona by my side. Tunbridge Wells was our first stop. "An unlikely place!" I hear you say. But it is an area full of splendid outcrops, well known in the climbing world, with such places as High Rocks, Bowles Outdoor Pursuit Centre, Toad Rocks, and the much loved Harrison's Rocks. These were our playground and made us feel like children again.

Arriving late one Sunday at High Rocks, a group of climbers, who were in fact about to pack up for the day, seeing that we were "greenhorns", devoted hours of their time to us, explaining the different routes. I have found this generosity to be characteristic of the climbing fraternity.

This small group was lead by a medium sized man in his mid-thirties called Gordon de Lacy. With a ready smile he introduced himself and his party. Then, in the twinkling of an eye, he shot up a very difficult pitch with great skill and power. Hanging almost upside down without a rope, he demonstrated the unseen holds. The rest of the party were good, but he was in a class of his own.

He confessed that he was only interested in outcrop and sea cliff climbing, with top roping his great joy. The great mountains held no interest for him. With boyish humour he called out the names of the various routes: Gaboon, Cobra, Possibility Wall, Pigs Nose, Inspiration and Fandango.

I improved considerably under his instruction, though never in a million years would I make a good climber. My physique weighed very much against me and was much more suited to judo, wrestling and the like. As long as there were big holds and easy, spectacular overhangs I was fine, and I could never resist the temptation to show off. This always sparked the comment from somewhere down below: "Oh, a boastful Toad!" Anything that required subtlety, however, exposed my inadequacies. Anyway, I didn't give a damn! I was having a wonderful time.

The climax of this happy period was a visit to Swanage in Dorset to attempt the 2,000-foot sea cliff climb, The Traverse of the Gods. With Gordon leading, we did it in five hours.

To complete the climb, you are required to swim a so-called Black Zawn and to ascend the easy cliffs on the other side, named Subliminal. This we duly did and were met at the top by a number of experienced climbers, who congratulated us warmly. I was dead chuffed and felt like a proper mountaineer. Though, somewhere in the wind, did I detect a small voice?

"Oh, a modest Toad."

In contrast to my previous trip, my return visit to Wales was relaxed and joyful. Geoff nodded his approval of my somewhat improved technique.

"Not bad at all, Sir Brian," sang his sweet Geordie voice. "But yer still have a tendency to forget to keep your heels down and there's no need to bomb up things — just take yer time, take yer time. In the city it's all rush, rush, rush. Here we learn to sit back and view things more calmly."

Indeed, the week spent with Geoff was deeply peaceful and full of humour and our ascent of Snowdon on this occasion was effortless and serene. The week cemented our friendship. Now I was a happy, confident Toad, eager for new horizons.

CHAPTER
THREE

The Sleeping Giant

In 1971 I had an adventure which gave me a great deal of happiness. In the spring of that year I found myself in Italy, playing the part of Pedro in the musical film *Man of La Mancha*, starring Peter O'Toole and Sophia Loren. This film took five months of my life but it did give me the opportunity to explore the wonderful Ibruzzi mountains.

Although I had spent so much time in the mountains, I had never been to any real altitude and this was something that I was longing to do. I needed to know if I might perhaps be one of those "mystical men who go high". It sounds fanciful, I know, but I was, and still am, guilty of a very romantic turn of phrase when pontificating about mountains and mountaineers.

Harry Dobson, my drama teacher from my early amateur days in Yorkshire, was once forced to interrupt me by quoting

> Mountaineers have furry ears,
> And pee through leather breeches,
> They wipe their arse on broken glass,
> Those hardy sons of bitches!

This timely reminder to curb my wilder excesses has always stayed with me and I often quote it when I find myself in full flow.

Man of La Mancha brought together a host of actors from England who were great chums. In addition, I had the privilege of making a number of fascinating new friends, including the brilliant choreographer, Gillian Lynne, and that fine American pianist and composer, Larry Rosenthal. Larry was forty-five years old, of medium height, slightly balding and with strong, sensitive dark eyes: "An artist to his finger tips". To give you some idea of his talent and stature, he wrote the music for such films as *Clash of the Titans* and *Becket*. Of course he was not the composer of *Man of La Mancha*; his job was to write some incidental music and to conduct the studio recording of the record. Most of the actors were not singers and his brief was to relax them and to give them confidence. He did just this and was much loved by all.

Larry resided in a lavish apartment, close by the Forum in Rome, having brought his lovely wife and two teenage daughters over from New York. My room, in a third-rate hotel near the Borghese Gardens, was extremely spartan by comparison, and I welcomed the opportunity to visit them. Within a short space of time, their apartment became my second home. The whole family was brimming with talent and I enjoyed many splendid musical evenings with them. I could ask Larry to play any piece of music that came to mind and he could always oblige. He was preparing for a demanding piano recital in Rome and I greatly appreciated my privileged position.

In perfect contrast to these artistic evenings, I also managed several visits to the Ibruzzi mountains. Whenever I could, I would find a guide in a remote little village and happily follow him, as he revealed the hidden wonders of that marvellous landscape. During this time, I also visited Pompeii and ascended Vesuvius. Sicily, too, was tantalisingly close, with its great volcano, Mount Etna. My determination to go there was absolute.

The whole area is alive with seismic activity and every square mile is steeped in legend. Stromboli is thought to be the Fire Island, which features in the wanderings of Odysseus. Following along the fault line, there is volcanic activity on the islands of Lipari and Vulcano; Vulcano being a hot, small steaming island, where springs of warm water energetically burst from hidden cracks to form gorgeous, stimulating pools to bathe in. This pulsating line then leads to Etna, where, underneath the mountain, the giant Encladeus sleeps, a sleepy titan who, whenever he changes position, causes an eruption.

During coffee breaks on the film set, the actors would love to listen to me rattling on about these wonders and they contributed their own love and knowledge of the region. Several of them wanted to join me in my exploits — exploits which would mean breaking their contracts, as it is absolutely forbidden in all film contracts to take part in any activity which might cause injury. Regardless of the risk, we made several treks into the Ibruzzi, ascending, by easy scramble routes, as many peaks as we could.

Of course, I took every care of them, carrying lots of gear, which always included a rope in perfect condition; I had seen too many people come a cropper with frayed ropes. One of the actors, John Castle, took to it all like a duck to water. Larry Rosenthal proved to be slow and methodical but always got there in the end. Gilly Lynne and some of her dancers were a revelation. Their agile and supple bodies overcame any difficulty with ease, first experience of height and exposure being the only problem. Gilly is probably the finest choreographer in the world and is also one of those rare people who can perform what they teach. On the rock faces, her physical dexterity made the Indian Rubber Man look stiff! It was only on descending that she experienced difficulty, stopping dead in her tracks and baulking at the prospect of descending scree slopes. "Oh dear, I don't like this, Golly!" (Golly was the nickname she had given me.) We tried so hard to look like Franz Klammer in our descent but I fancy we looked more like Godzilla and Godzukki!

The final upshot of these excursions was that Larry said he wanted to accompany me to Sicily when I went to climb Mount Etna. The signs were good. The film was to break for a five-day holiday period at Easter, and planes flew regularly from Rome to Sicily, taking only three-quarters of an hour to get there. The scene was set for our little expedition.

As the appointed time grew near, Larry started looking

for reasons not to go. The most feeble of these excuses concerned his dog, Bentley, whom he had brought with him from the States. "My family is going away," he groaned, "I'm worried about Bentley!"

But I had made up my mind — he was coming with me! "For God's sake, Larry!" I replied. "We've been over this time and time again. You know very well that we've arranged a lovely kennel for him. He's going to share a nice lawned area with a lovely female — the Italians are catering for his every need! We'll only be away for two days. No one loves Bentley more than I do!"

This was perfectly true. Bentley was a big, black, bushy old dog, who farted and growled at everybody and stank to high-heaven. (Larry didn't believe that he should be bathed, as he felt he would lose his oils.) God only knows why, but Bentley loved me and melted visibly when I appeared.

I hasten to add that he was the most over-sexed, rampant dog I have ever seen, sporting a chopper the like of which would not shame an elephant! When he finally arrived at the aforementioned kennels, he didn't give us a backward glance, as he powered his way towards his new female companion. "Ah!" sighed the large, jovial Italian in charge. "Zay get on very well. It is love at first sight!"

Anyway, after a great deal of pushing, cajoling, pleading and shouting, I somehow managed to spirit Larry onto the plane. At last I had him where I wanted him and strapped him into his seat. During the flight, I managed to calm him down with encouraging words of cheer. But, alas, his confidence evaporated completely when he clapped eyes on Etna, in the fading evening light.

"My God, Brian!" he whispered in awe. "Just look at it!"

The plane made a spectacular circle around Etna, veering close to its sides. The mountain was dark and sinister with a surprising amount of snow and ice on its flanks. Periodically, in weird contrast, tongues of fire shot out from red fumuroles on the strange, twisted summit cone. Larry's apprehension increased.

"God, Brian! How on earth are we going to get up there!"

"Step by step, Larry," was my reply, though I must confess that my feelings were actually not dissimilar to his. The cataracts and fumuroles were a complete surprise. They certainly were not mentioned in the Michelin Tyre Motor Brochure!

To add to all this, on arriving at Catania, we were informed by reliable sources that the terrain of the mountain varied from week to week, depending on the flow of the lava. All this information cheered Larry to no end, as he sat in stony silence pondering it all.

I ignored his gloom and bundled him into the hired car. We sped away towards our smoky objective, our destination for that night being the Sapienza Refuge, situated at the base of the mountain at 6,000 feet. I understand now that it no longer exists, having been swept away after a major eruption!

It was a large wooden building, with a bar, a small restaurant and numerous bedrooms, each containing several bunk beds. The atmosphere was warm and friendly, due mainly to the *bonhomie* of our tubby, jolly host.

"You are fortunate!" he hooted. "The mountain iss ahh — ow do you say — iss-a-quiet. Zee giant under ze top iss asleep. You climb quietly, you won't wake him. Zen we all live to see tomorrow, eh?"

He then laughed uncontrollably. But this *joie de vivre* was wasted on Larry. His worried eyes searched mine for any expression of doubt, but I just slapped him on the back to jolly him along.

Fortunately, there was an old guide who resided at the refuge and he was able to give me some sensible advice as to which route to take. He would gladly have come with us, but his services had been booked by someone else on a different part of the mountain.

He advised me to walk alongside the cable cars, which ended at about 7,000 feet, and then to proceed left on fairly easy ground. From there, he maintained, the route was safe and obvious, but we should not veer away from it. His only reservation was that there had been a fair amount of unseasonal snow, which had covered some of the pot holes, these being six to eight feet deep. He said that I should beware of the gases on the summit cone, and use common sense and not climb into the streaming smoke pouring out from the top.

His wrinkled face then broke into a smile. The great mountain usually went to sleep at midday, he informed me. The volumes of black smoke turned grey, then white and gradually diminished, ultimately disappearing altogether. But, be warned, they start up again in mid-afternoon.

I thanked him for his kindness and said goodnight. Larry and I retired to our respective bunk beds, set the alarm for 2 a.m. and fell asleep. At 3 a.m. the next morning, suitably dressed and with a seventy-foot rope tied securely to Larry, I led the way up the ancient lava of Etna.

It was cold — just above freezing. The stars thronged the sky, giving cheer to our laboured efforts, as we progressed steadily towards the final tower of the cable cars at 7,000 feet.

My occasional enquiry of Larry, as to how he was, received a positive nod. His bright clothes showed up against the sombre background and far away the lights of Catania lit up the morning, making one feel less lonely. With perfect timing, as we arrived at the tower, dawn broke and filled us with a feeling of well-being and anticipation.

The black landscape became multi-coloured. The sun's rays moved dramatically and rapidly uphill, revealing the mountain's secrets. A vast panorama of snow fields, ridges, gullies and smoking hot vents all pointed the way to the pyramid and final summit cone. This last obstacle was dark and twisted, its features reminding me of Sycarax, the hideous mother of the monster Grendel, in the story of Beowulf. For a while the vista looked like a scene from Dante's *Inferno*; that is, until the full power of the sun embraced it.

With arms around each others' shoulders, Larry and I watched the sunrise like newborn babies. That wondrous golden orb gave its warmth and light to every nook and cranny of the volcano, banishing its former quality and transforming it to a thing of haunting beauty. Nothing was said, all was silent and still.

We sat down to drink coffee from our flasks, to put cream on our faces and to don our dark glasses. Our new-found friend, the sun, needed to be handled with respect; the large amount of snow, reflecting its rays, would soon play havoc with our eyes.

Larry was happier now and we made fine progress through the snow fields. After an hour or so, we found ourselves within about 1,000 feet of the final rocky pyramid. Then I felt a tug on my waist as the rope tightened slightly. Looking back, I saw Larry up to his neck in snow. I secured an anchor and strode down towards him.

"Am I supposed to be like this, Brian?" he enquired.

Unable to suppress my laughter, I said, "It's all part of life's rich pattern, Larry!" and I began to dig with my hands to pull him out.

Of course, it all seemed harmless fun but five people that year had disappeared on Etna. "Swallowed up" was the term used by the Sicilians. (This little titbit of information I withheld from Larry.)

Our progress took us to 10,000 feet, the highest that I and, needless to say, Larry had ever been. Our excitement knew no bounds. We could discern the curvature of the earth. The width at the base of the volcano is eighty-nine miles and we could feel its roots reaching powerfully through the countryside, influencing all. Oh yes, there was no doubt that the mighty titan, Encladeus, resided under it!

"Be still, giant," I thought. "No eruptions today." After all, I had been informed that on occasions when the fellow did awaken, resulting lava flows from the side and main vents could exceed sixty miles an hour. This was another piece of information I did not reveal to my gallant companion.

After progressing some hundred feet, Larry quite suddenly stopped and expressed a wish to talk to his parents, who he said were standing by his side.

"Fine, Larry, fine," I replied. "Tell them not to stay too long, though, as I wish to get you up to the summit by midday and down again before the afternoon clouds gather."

Later, I was to discover from him that his parents had died together in a car crash some years before. Looking down on him, a little distance away, he was quietly conversing with them and I found myself diplomatically turning away to give him some privacy. After a short time, I felt the rope tugging in my hand and Larry informed me that he was ready to continue.

Etna is almost 11,000 feet high and the final pyramid at that time had a sixty degree slope, which had us both panting. The combination of hot sun and roasting volcano forced us to shed most of our outer garments.

On finally arriving at the summit, we embraced in triumph then tried to find a cool place to sit down. This proved nigh on impossible, as each resting place was so hot it singed our trousers. We hopped from boulder to boulder, seeking out one that might be tolerable and giggled like schoolboys.

The ascent had worked out splendidly, but I insisted that we stay no more than half an hour on the top, as the old guide back at the refuge had said the weather conditions could change considerably in the afternoon. We explored the lip of the main crater and several small calderas that lead from it. And then, as we had been told, the volcano did indeed go to sleep. The black smoke turned grey, then white and finally disappeared.

Remembering the guide's words, I seized the opportunity. Keeping the rope tight on Larry and securing myself to boulders, I manipulated him into a safe position from where he could peer down into the cauldron, a handkerchief protecting his nose and mouth. His curiosity satisfied, I pulled him back and took his place. I was stunned by the sight that greeted me a hundred feet below. A small lake of hot lava gently rose and fell, as if breathing to some ancient tune. Periodically and within seconds, its surface appeared to cool and develop a skin streaked with blue veins that formed a tapestry of subtle shapes. Then, in an instant, it would be destroyed again by the consuming fires of the hotter lava down below.

"That's what the Earth looked like three thousand million years ago," I thought. "All life started in this primordial way." My face began to feel the heat and I hastily, but regretfully, pulled back from this awesome work of nature and wondered if I would ever see its like again.

We looked about us at the primitive landscape, ate

our chocolate and slowly drank our coffee, unable to say a word. We experienced an atavistic feeling that the cauldron of overwhelming heat, containing that dreadful vortex of boiling molten lava, was, nevertheless, not alien to the chemistry of our own bodies. Instead, it gave us a strange feeling of belonging, as if there was nothing to fear.

Without a doubt, to climb this wondrous giant volcano, the largest in Europe, was a deep and unique experience. I was so happy for Larry as, for him, the effort was like going to the moon. If I had little or no talent for mountaineering, he had less, and so his achievement is a bench-mark in my book by which to measure the endeavours of others and indeed my own! I was greatly moved by what he had done, and his face positively glowed with pride and satisfaction.

The time was 1 p.m. when we started our descent. This went smoothly enough, despite the expected cloud, which rapidly sped up the mountain. Descending puts a strain on muscles that one doesn't ordinarily use and can cause irritation, particularly when combined with a long day and altitude. It was precisely this that compelled Larry to question my judgement, as he ventured tentatively.

"I think you're wrong, Brian. We should be turning right."

"No Larry. It's another 500 yards, then we'll see the tower of the cable cars on the left. Try to keep quiet, the altitude is making you irritable."

He nodded and accepted what I had said and, lo and behold, the friendly shape of the tower loomed up. I hasten to add that my route finding was aided by my compass. The cable cars were now working and took us down 2,000 feet to the security of the Sapienza Refuge.

Arriving at 4 p.m. we decided to sleep for a few hours, then to have dinner and set off for Rome the next morning. Our meal that evening was quiet and reflective. A fire filled the room with its cheer and warmth and the flickering flames highlighted the faces of two friends contentedly drinking red wine; the red wine from the vines growing on the black soil of Mount Etna; *Lachryma Christi* — The Tears of Christ.

Two weeks later, back in Larry's apartment in Rome, I found myself fidgeting nervously, as he seemed to be having difficulty with a complicated piece of music that he was practising for his grand solo concert in the Eternal City. On the appointed day, a large expectant audience of 2,000 or more filled the concert hall to overflowing. Never had I experienced such fear for a fellow artist! I had on many occasions felt "first night nerves" for another actor, but at least I fully understood what they were going through. Larry, in contrast, was a pianist. His art was strange and mysterious to me and seemed terrifyingly difficult.

Larry made his entrance, smartly dressed in an evening suit, but his face looked haggard and pale. I shrank into my chair, consumed with nerves. The auditorium dimmed, the applause died down and, in customary silence, 2,000 people focused on the pianist and his piano. My fists bit into the sides of my cushioned chair and I held my breath.

I might as well have spared myself the pain; his

fingers hit the piano with stunning power, as if his life depended on it. The strength and certainty of his playing electrified the audience. He was performing a Japanese piece that I had never heard before. "You crafty old sod!" I thought. "You hid this from me!"

I relaxed as he swept on in triumph. Passion, humour, tenderness — it was all there. The evening became a happening. The audience rose as one and bellowed their lungs out in appreciation. In the mayhem that followed, I spirited myself away, scuttling like a demented crab through the dark side streets, seeking their cloaking darkness. Larry's stupendous artistry had rendered me uncomfortably shy. Also, I was overwhelmed with a sense of guilt.

Having put a suitable distance between me and the concert hall, I found myself sitting in the gutter, staring out into the hot, humid Roman night. After half an hour or so, I felt a hand on my shoulder. Turning, I found Larry's concerned, sensitive face smiling at me.

"Brian . . . Brian . . . Are you all right? What are you doing here? I've been looking everywhere for you. Didn't you like the concert?"

For the next twenty minutes, I tried to explain to him that I was overcome by his performance, and that I was utterly ashamed that I had irresponsibly taken him climbing, putting such a dreadful strain on his precious pianist's fingers. "I had no idea, Larry," I choked, "that you could play like that. Never, in a million years, would I have taken you rock climbing."

Larry put an arm round me, saying, "Brian, dear Brian. Climbing Mount Etna is arguably the finest achievement of my life. I can never thank you enough for taking me. You wouldn't want me to have missed it, would you?"

He then rubbed my head and continued, "Come on. Let's go to the Trevi Fountain and have a hot chocolate!"

CHAPTER
FOUR

White Mountain, Red Feet

The year was now 1972. The experience of Mount Etna fired me with new energy to ascend the high peaks and, inevitably, the Alps beckoned. John Miller, my theatrical agent, was none too pleased about it, voicing his concern for my safety. He also pointed out that such activities took a great deal of time, frequently rendering me unavailable for work.

In spite of all this, he always backed me up, displaying a warmth and sympathy that I greatly appreciated. On learning that I was buzzing off for five weeks, for my first Alpine season, he nodded his head fatalistically. "You daft old sod!" he said smiling.

The plan was that I should meet up with Geoff Arkless's wife, Breda, and their six children in Ramsgate, Kent. We would then take the ferry to Dieppe and I would drive them in their van through France to Saas Fee in Switzerland for the start of the season. Geoff would join us there, after completing a climb with a client on Monte Rosa.

At this time I was just finishing a play for ATV called *Reflections*. It was a romantic tale in the popular *Love Story* series, and I played Andrew Kefford, a character based loosely on the explorer Fawcett who had disappeared during an expedition in South America. I greatly enjoyed this rare opportunity to play a lover, with the added bonus of the lovely Susanne Neve as my leading lady. As soon as the play was enjoyably concluded I made haste for Ramsgate.

Breda Arkless is one of Britain's leading lady climbers — her reputation second to none. Therefore, it was a complete surprise, on arriving at the port, to find her sporting a large pot on her leg. Her pretty, cherubic face contorted with embarrassment. "Would you believe it, Brian! All the dangerous mountains I've climbed, and I go and break my leg slipping off the step outside the kitchen door — a height of five inches!" Her positive nature, however, made light of it all, as we cheerfully organised the children into the van.

The channel crossing went smoothly enough and I was surprised how quickly we then progressed through France. Towns and villages simply whizzed by. The weather was fine and the evening ritual of pitching the tents in some farmer's field was pure fun of the chaotic kind. Once the youngsters were washed and had hot drinks in their hands, they would turn their eager faces to me for the evening fairy story.

These stories ranged from "Rumpelstiltskin" to the much loved "Pinnochio". Oh, how they loved them all, their eyes getting bigger by the minute as I described the size of the great whale, Monstero. To get them into bed

49

proved almost impossible for Breda, as "Oh, tell us some more, Mr Brian!" was the frequent plea. ("Mr Brian" was the name they had given me from the beginning of the trip, and it had stuck.)

"I'll give you one more story if you're in your sleeping bags in two minutes!"

Then, before you could say Jack Robinson, they were tucked away in their respective cocoons, and I employed my softest voice and gentlest story to ease them into the land of nod.

By the time we arrived in the valley of Saas Fee, my fund of tales was nearing exhaustion. As I still had several weeks of story telling to go, I dreamed up permutations of the originals, which fortunately proved more than acceptable. In the history of story telling, I doubt whether Scheherazade herself could have been more searchingly tested!

Now that we were in Switzerland, my excitement knew no bounds. The mountains were not visible from the valley but my impatience to see them gave wings to my feet and I raced up the hillside for a glimpse of their grandeur.

On my return, I poured out to Breda my impressions with enthusiastic vigour. All the while she nodded and smiled, pleased that my experience had made me so happy, at the same time unable to hide her disappointment at not being able to accompany me.

"Ah, come on!" I urged her. "To hell with your broken leg! There's a lovely, easy rock face out there. Let's go and climb it!"

Half an hour later, in my usual gorilla-type style, I led

the way to the top of the 150-foot face with an extra long rope, and belayed securely to the top.

"Not quite in Mallory's style, eh Breda?" I shouted. "Okay, let's be having you. Up yer come!"

She fastened on the rope with a bowline, gave me a quick look, and insisted that I put on my belay gloves. "I won't move until you do, Brian."

Then, satisfied that all was in order, she made her first tentative move. "Oh, Brian," she whispered. "I don't know as I should be doing this."

"Ah, Breda," I replied. "With your ability, you'll eat it, broken leg and all!"

Even with the disadvantage of a large pot on her leg, she moved gracefully and easily up the face: a little pressure here, a side-hold there, all delightful to observe, her face all the while expressing delight to be on the rock again. Then, at last, seated alongside me and taking in the scenery, she gave a contented sigh.

I've failed to mention that we also had a twenty-year-old girl in our party, named Jane, who was a friend of the Arkless family. She was like a youthful aunt to the children, which allowed Breda to make the odd sortie with me.

Geoff still hadn't arrived and Breda, noting that I was kicking my heels, suggested that I join Jane to climb the easy and accessible mountain, the Metaghorn. This we did, after a leisurely three-hour walk along a rough, winding, well-used pathway. Though a modest excursion, I felt happy and exhilarated — after all, it was my first Alpine peak.

It was good to be at 10,000 feet again, our eyes

feasting on the vast range of mountains, with the impressive Allalinhorn looming over all. Our attention was drawn to a large glacier at the base of our mountain, which lead the way to the higher peaks. Several climbers could be seen crossing it on a clear track through the snow to a distant large wooden building. This, we were informed by a passer-by, was the Britannia Hut where we would be assured of plenty of hot soup and brown bread. It all sounded very inviting and, besides, the routes across the glacier looked great fun.

The hour was young; we had climbed the Metaghorn and it was still only 10 a.m. Our spirits were up, and we decided to push on. A mistake! In our ignorance, we underestimated the distance and the time the journey would take. The snow also proved to be heavy and deep. But we ploughed on and after several hours, the welcome sight of our objective came into view.

On this occasion the Britannia Hut lived up to its name, seemingly full to the brim with Great Britons.

"Hello, Brian. How are you?"

"What's an actor doing up here?"

"Can we buy you a drink, Brian, lad?"

I have always found it gratifying that the public regard me as one of them and not as some vague figure, aloof from the world, living in some country retreat (though I do!). "Brian" is what everybody calls me and I'm glad that they do. In Britannia huge bowls of soup were placed in front of us and such was our thirst from dehydration, that we drank it like thirsty horses, syphoning it away inch by inch.

I eagerly interrogated other climbers about their

experiences and made no note of time passing, absorbed as I was in their stories which they told with such love for their subject.

Inevitably, we arrived at the disappearance of Mallory and Irvine on Everest in 1924, and the Britannia Hut bore witness to an impassioned debate as to what had actually happened to our revered heroes. Some thought they climbed the mountain, others voiced grave doubts. In the end they all felt it was better not to know and that it should remain a mystery and so retain its romance and fascination.

Three Scottish climbers, with tired faces, witnessed the end of this discussion and asked for the whole story to be recounted; they had never heard of Mallory and Irvine. Liberal amounts of warm wine had loosened everyone's inhibitions and as all faces turned to me I endeavoured, as accurately as possible, to tell the tale. The atmosphere was charged with emotion and, talking slowly and quietly, I built up the story, painstakingly introducing the characters and events and moving remorselessly to the inevitable climax; ending with Ruth Mallory's words, describing her feelings about her husband's death, in a letter to Geoffrey Withrope-Young.

I know George did not mean to be killed; he meant not to be so hard that I did not a bit think he would be. I don't think I do feel that his death makes me the least proud of him. It is his life that I loved and love. I know so absolutely that he could not have failed in courage or self-sacrifice. Whether he got to the top of the mountain or did not, whether he lived or died makes no difference to my admiration for him. I think I have got the pain separate. There is so much of it, and it will go on so long, that I must do that. Oh, Geoffrey. If it hadn't happened! It might so easily might not have.

It is difficult for me to believe that George's spirit was ready for another life, and his way of going to it was very beautiful. I don't think this pain matters at all, I have had far more than my share of joy, and always shall have had.

Isn't it queer how all the time what matters most is to get hold of the rightness of things? Then some sort of peace comes.

On completing these words, as they say in the theatre, "there wasn't a dry eye in the house". Our Scottish friends were particularly shaken. The power of Ruth Mallory's sentiments had affected them deeply in their exhausted state.

"It would make a great film," someone said tentatively in the ensuing silence. My fate was sealed.

"Go on, Brian. Film their journey; follow in their footsteps. Put it on film. They're being forgotten."

I promised to do everything in my power to bring it about, at the same time I knew how impossible it really was. But their enthusiasm was catching and a tiny seed was planted in my brain. In the same instant I cast it out, telling myself the whole idea was ridiculous. Go to Mount Everest, indeed! How daft! Obtain permits; book climbers, doctors, logistic managers, equipment, porters,

Sherpas, Yak herders, camera crews; not to mention the huge budget that would be involved! Still, there was no harm in romancing and a good time was had by all.

It was not until I felt Jane tugging at my sleeve that I realised how late it was; there were barely three hours of daylight left. We said our goodbyes and, without further ado, sped along a straight path beneath a blue ice wall towards the cable car, which we understood would be shortly closing. But, although our journey took only twenty minutes, we missed the last car by a whisker.

"Never mind. There's a straight, rocky path down towards the valley. It shouldn't take long."

Another miscalculation! The valley was a good 5,000 feet below us, and by the time we descended a couple of thousand feet, the sun had long since disappeared behind the mountains. The last part of the journey proved hard and tricky and was not helped by the fact that I'd neglected to take my headlamp. But, worst of all, my damned right foot was giving me hell.

It has been deformed from birth. In shape it isn't so bad, simply displaying a badly fallen arch. The base of the ankle is the problem; it is bent, throwing the foot out almost at right angles. Also, I have very strong bones in contrast to my skin, which is weak. Therefore, the bone breaks the skin and this was what was happening on this descent, soaking my socks with blood. I hear you say, "Try this, try that, Brian." I can only reply that I have tried everything, including salts, powders, lotions and powerful brine.

The latter was suggested to me in 1964 by the legendary ex-heavyweight champion of the world, Jack

Dempsey. He and I were guests of the New York police (Z-Cars, need I say), and he informed me that from his earliest years he had soaked his face in brine every day and had never lost a fight through cuts. Unfortunately, Dempsey's remedy proved as ineffective in my case as the rest.

My feet continue to give me problems but, by painstaking efforts, I somehow manage to keep the weakness reasonably controlled. On this particular descent I discovered that my footwear was also wrong. I was wearing hard leather climbing boots, which are not really suitable for scrambling or walking. After taking good advice and, by a process of elimination, I have managed over the years to ease the problem. (Incidentally, boots made to measure are particularly disastrous.) Footwear is vitally important and the wrong choice can spoil a holiday or expedition. George Leigh Mallory himself, describing an attempt on Everest, laid emphasis on this: "Even so small a thing as a boot fitting a shade too tight may endanger a man's foot, and involve the whole party in a complete descent."

That evening, when Jane and I finally arrived back at camp in Saas Fee, Long John Silver would have been proud of me. Feeling like a naughty school boy, I was confronted by Breda's pale concerned face.

"Where have you been? Do you realise you have been gone for twelve hours! It's nearly 9 p.m. I've been going frantic, sending people out to look for you everywhere. I expected you back by lunchtime!"

Deeply embarrassed and utterly confounded, I shame-facedly described our adventures.

"My God, Geoff!" she exclaimed. "They've crossed the glacier!"

In my bemused state, I had failed to see Geoff. He had completed his climb on Monte Rosa and had arrived earlier than expected. There was a suggestion of a smile on his thin, drawn face as he came forward into the firelight.

"Well, Mr Blessed — or should I call you Sir Brian. Your fame, it seems, follows you even to the Britannia Hut but not, it would seem, your brains! Crossing glaciers is a very serious business, even for the most experienced mountaineers but not for Mr Blessed who, like the Lord Jesus Christ, thinks he can walk on water!

"Please try and use some common sense. When Breda trusts you to go to the Metaghorn and to return in reasonable time, then you must do as you are told. Now you've overdone it and are hobbling about like an old man. With that kind of brainpower, it makes me wonder how you learn your lines."

Of course, Geoff and Breda are the kindest people in the world and, once the disciplining was over, they made oodles of tea to combat our dehydration. They then examined my foot with concern.

"Dear me," said Geoff. "Thank God we're leaving Saas Fee for Chamonix tomorrow. This will give your foot a few days' rest and a chance to recover. I'm afraid, Sir Brian, it is doubtful if you'll be able to do any of the big climbs with it in that state."

"Don't you believe it!" I replied. "I don't intend it to stop me from climbing!"

Geoff smiled. "Ah, I see we have a masochist in our midst!"

As I soaked my feet in hot salt water and devoured her delicious stew, Breda whispered in my ear that the children had fought off sleep in the hope that I would return and tell them a story. There they were in a large tent, lying in their sleeping bags, beaming faces lit up with expectation. The overhead lamp rocked gently to and fro and all was cosy and warm.

"Could we have a story, Mr Brian?"

As I settled myself down and was about to begin, I became aware that three more children, disguised as Breda, Geoff and Jane, had surreptitiously joined my audience. When all was still and concentration absolute, I broke the silence: "Tonight's story is called 'The King of The Golden River'."

On arriving in Chamonix the next day, we found absolute chaos; the beetling town throbbed with the energy of climbers, skiers, walkers and tourists. "Look! Look! You can see Mont Blanc! The highest mountain in Europe!" "Western Europe," came the corrective.

The entire town seemed to pay homage to the great white mountain. The air was keen and fresh, with a purity that washed every brain cell, and I couldn't help being caught up in the vibrancy that abounded.

Tough mountaineers strode purposefully through the streets, stopping to examine some piece of equipment or to consult a map.

Some sported broken arms and legs, others, puffed up with pride, showed off their frost-bitten toes, achieved whilst ascending the Brenva Route on Mont Blanc in storm conditions.

The woods on the outskirts of the town were chock-a-block with multi-coloured tents, occupied by happy conquistadors, their eyes and hearts ambitiously set on the surrounding giants. A stream ran through the encampment and we found ourselves a convenient place alongside it. My tent was dark blue and designed for two people, although, in actual fact, I had difficulty squeezing into it alone! Viewed from the outside, climbers would, on occasion, be astonished at its peculiar, bulging shape; but it was only that I had visitors and that it was story time again!

Breda could never understand why her children, on story days, had diminished appetites. The crumbs, licked out jam jars and chocolate papers in my tent could easily have cleared up the mystery, but my lips were sealed. "No names, no pack-drill" was the order of the day.

One day, ten climbers joined our party. They arrived with Geoff's climbing partner, eager to embark on their Alpine season. This was a bit disconcerting, as they were obviously streets ahead of me in ability, experience and fitness. At least my foot was slowly responding to treatment.

After friendly introductions at dawn the next day, I found myself, suitably dressed and carrying my rucksack, accompanying them to our first climb. It was a mountain named "M", quite close to Les Drus, and so called because in shape it closely resembles that letter. Geoff was our leader and our ascent would take us to about 10,000 or 11,000 feet.

We took the cable car to 9,000 feet, disembarked and moved at a rate of knots over glaciers, rocks and streams until after an hour or so we arrived at our destination. It was reassuring to note that my companions were as out of breath as I was, sweat pouring freely as we savoured the view and our first good drink.

My foot was holding out, thank God, although it was covered with elastoplasts and lashings of vaseline. Geoff observed me with quiet humour.

"Well, Mr Blessed, I'll bet that made you cough a bit! So what do you think of the climb you are facing?"

I replied that it looked hard.

"Ah, it's not as hard as it looks," he said. "The hardest bit is the thin chimney, which you can lay back on, and the pitch above. In all, it's about 'severe standard'. The top pitches ease off. It's no harder than anything you've done in Wales or Swanage — just different because of the altitude. Take yer time."

One of the members of our party was a stocky, attractive young lady, the only woman amongst us, who had surprised me with her turn of speed across the glaciers. Over the years I have learned not to judge people by their appearances. The said lady was a fine example, her movements being fluent and agile. In contrast, one of the men, looking perfectly like a mountaineer — tall, slim and strong — was as stiff as a board.

When climbing in the Alps, it comes as a shock to see how many people there are on the different routes. One has to rise very early to get to the front of the queue. Now I understood why we had dashed across the glaciers

— all in vain I'm afraid, for there were several parties ahead of us. Fortunately, most of them were already high on the face.

After we had completed the first pitch, we found a party of four Japanese in front of us, who were having difficulty with the narrow chimney that Geoff mentioned. I have never seen climbers wearing such colourful gear! Their clothes reflected the early morning sun, as they tried to come to terms with the tricky second pitch. Yellow and red ropes hung haphazardly down the rock, jamming and tangling in the thin cracks. The lead climber from the land of the rising sun was squirming about trying to free his leg, which was firmly stuck in the chimney, all the while letting out painful cries. *"Itie! Itie!"* (Ouch! Ouch!)

Two members of the group endeavoured to pull him free, all to no avail. He screamed louder and aimed punches at them. Then, all activities ceased and the wily orientals gathered around their leader in quiet meditation. At this point, Geoff informed us that he would lead us around the "yellow peril" on a less interesting and easier pitch, otherwise we would be there for the duration.

Over the next two hours, he led us calmly and easily up the climb, until, at last, there were only two pitches to go. The first was about eighty feet and Geoff disappeared from view as he completed it. Minutes later, he shouted that he was taking in slack and I followed him, with the traditional call of "Climbing".

Within seconds, I was aware of a climber approaching me on my left. It was another Japanese team, attempting a different route, and the lead climber had similarities in style to the previous oriental gentleman! I was amazed to see him clip his karabena into ours, eight feet below me, and to storm feverishly upwards, seeking to grip my feet! He was in a state of total panic and unable to find any decent holds. A strange whining sound came from his lips, which turned to paroxysms of mad glee when he perceived his salvation: fifteen stone of Brian Blessed and a rope! Before you could say "Bob's Yer Uncle", he pulled himself alongside me by way of my feet, trousers, belt and shoulders.

There, on the mountain "M", East and West met face to face. All hell broke loose as we swung dangerously, pendulum like, on the vertical 2,000-foot face. Holding on to my rope with my left hand, I held the demented Samurai firmly with the other and, with utter rage at his unseemly behaviour, shook his small body like a rag doll. At the same time, evolution-wise, I put myself beyond redemption by my atavistic ravings. I am quite convinced that that choice French author, Rabelais himself, who wrote those rustic exploits of the giants Gargantua and Pantagruel, would have found my language unacceptable.

It was only when I observed Tojo's face (for that was the name I had given him) turning a shade of red, that I realised what pressure his wind pipe was under. With a voice that echoed around the surrounding peaks, I recommended that he either take a running jump or rapidly ascend the rope above me and disappear from my sight forever. He seemed to understand this and scuttled upwards like an animated mushroom.

Peace at last, I thought, as I prepared to ascend. Not so. My social life expanded again, as a second nip tentatively approached my feet. My hospitality to my previous visitor had been noted, and now the gentlest of hands held my feet, while the other gesticulated appeasement and supplication. Buddha himself would have been moved to shower him with myriads of lotus flowers.

The mighty Alpinist, Blessed, at first viewed him with lofty disdain, which, after a few seconds of self-examination, turned to pity and remorse, as I finally exclaimed, "Ah, come on, son. Grab my hand."

In that instant, I recognised a man who was as inexperienced and as vulnerable on the mountain as myself. As he came alongside me, I nodded as affably as I could and encouraged him to climb up by using the rope. After what seemed an eternity, the second exponent of the art of Hari Kari gradually left my sight.

Geoff's face, when I reached him, was as enigmatic as the sphinx. "You didn't tell me you were bringing friends! Anyway, Mr Blessed, you can lead the last pitch yourself, it's quite easy and straightforward."

The summit at last! There, to my surprise, were the two Japanese. They greeted me enthusiastically, squealing and grinning with delight and hopping up and down. Patting me affectionately on the back, they poured me coffee and pumped a good supply of biscuits into my hands. Their glee knew no bounds when the one I had half throttled, made valiant attempts to imitate my actions and voice. They actually seemed to honour my appalling behaviour. Either that or they were simply overwhelmingly relieved to have climbed the mountain. Ah, well! I thought, all's well that ends well! The rest of our party duly arrived on the large summit and we all bathed luxuriously in the Alpine sun.

During the next few weeks we did a variety of climbs, which satisfied all tastes. One in particular, however, brought back fears that I had experienced when first climbing in Wales.

The objective was L'Aiguille du Midi, which involved a long ridge climb, culminating with a descent of the vast Mer de Glace. We were the usual party of a dozen or so and the first part of the adventure was easy enough; a journey by cable car from Chamonix to the Midi at 12,000 feet.

L'Aiguille du Midi is a wonderfully impressive fortress, like a castle of granite with rock spires pointing skywards. Here the cable car comes to a stop and there are tables, chairs, food and drink to be had. So, for a modest fee, people who have never climbed can go 12,000 feet and gaze at nearby Mont Blanc and the other wonderful peaks.

All this is perfectly sedate and secure. It is only when one ventures out onto the ridges that the atmosphere changes quite abruptly to the realm of ice-axes, ropes, karabenas, ice-screws, winds, exposure and daunting precipices.

Our climb on knife-edge ridges towards the distant Travi-de-Plan took much longer than we expected; the winds were keen and our progress slow. On both sides the steep slopes looked threatening and ominous. If someone slipped in front or behind, one must instantly counterbalance it by throwing oneself on the opposite side of the ridge. It was interesting to note that now, after several weeks of climbing ridges, my fears of them had somewhat decreased and I had begun to enjoy them; without ever even for one moment losing my respect for the dangers they posed.

With about a quarter of a mile to go, Geoff decided that it was getting too late to complete the climb, so he led us down the steep slopes towards the famous Mer-de-Glace. The sun was now high in the sky, beating down on us and reflecting back up again off the snow and ice. I was astonished at how savage the heat actually was. We were compelled to cover every pore of our faces with suncream and to put on balaclavas. We poured with sweat and removed all outer garments. After this torture, we found ourselves on the threshold of the mighty glacier.

One of the climbers, Charlie, was training to be a guide, so Geoff told him to lead us down through the chaos of the glacier. God in Heaven! The whole process was murder! The poor lad performed creditably but at times was totally bemused by the sea of snow and hidden dangers and by Geoff's constant nagging. "Not that way Charlie! Think man, think! Look at the ice. It's blue all around you. No, no, no! You're leading us straight towards the awful crevasse! Don't just bomb ahead. Work it out, study the terrain, then move."

Descending puts a strain on muscles you don't normally use and we were fighting off dehydration and suffering severe headaches. Geoff's carping voice felt like someone rubbing sandpaper over my naked brains! So I intervened.

"For God's sake, Geoff! You lead the bloody climb or we'll be here forever!"

His measured reply put me firmly in my place. "Mr Blessed, when I tell you how to play Shakespeare, you can tell me how to climb!"

I sheepishly nodded my head and offered my apologies to Charlie, who wouldn't have been put out if Geoff had acceded to my request. Charlie was now standing on a promontory of hard snow, looking out over a daunting ravine immediately below him.

"What do I do, Geoff?" he enquired plaintively.

"Jump! Bloody jump!" Geoff replied. "Don't hang about, I'm standing on a bergshund. That serac overlooking us is making clicking sounds, which means it's about to fall over, so bloody jump!"

The trainee guide did just that and we all followed swiftly. This procedure went on for hours and we were all scared witless. George Leigh Mallory, like most mountaineers, made light of this glacier when talking about it, describing how he would break off for lunch or tiffin and nonchalantly make his way to the base of it. In contrast, I must say, I was shaking with fear, the constant leaping, unroped, across what Geoff called simple crevasses quite unnerved me.

The sun was now losing its power and a cold wind embraced us, so we put our outer garments on again quickly, as the sweat on our bodies was freezing. Then, at last, the undulating folds of ice pointed the way to our exit rocks and the agony was over. As I sat outside a wooden hut alongside the glacier, it took all my willpower to control myself. I found myself shaking feverishly.

When at last some semblance of calm returned, Geoff appeared with a huge mug of hot coffee, laced with sugar and Nestle's milk. For just a moment his hand brushed my head. "All right, Brian?" he said quietly. "I thought it best to leave you alone for a while."

The next day, back at camp, I viewed my right foot with horror. The long descent of La Mer de Glace had taken its toll; you could see the bone clearly through a large wound in my heel, and my instep was covered with open blisters and bad lacerations. The ball of my foot had bled badly and I had problems with my toes. "God! Oh God!" I thought. "If only I had good feet!"

Throughout the day I watched jealously as climbers, on returning to their tents, soaked their strong feet in the stream. Feet, it seemed to me, that had never seen a blister! Given my condition, Geoff and Breda both felt it was unwise for me to even consider climbing any more that season. Breda was kindness itself and suggested that in future I should allow a specialist to make me boots to measure.

I leaned back against my rucksack, watching the flames of the camp fire and appreciating the hot salt water Breda had prepared for my feet. I knew that, in two days' time, other climbers would be joining the group, the intention being to attempt the highest mountain, Mont Blanc.

Oh, how I wanted to climb it, to follow in Mallory's footsteps. In spite of all the horrors of the previous day,

I was determined to achieve this. With my foot in its present condition, Geoff thought it out of the question, but he left the final decision to me.

"Then I will go, Geoff!" I proclaimed. "Nothing will stop me!"

He nodded fatalistically and muttered quietly as he moved away for his evening walk. "You've more guts than sense."

Finding myself alone I snuggled up and closed my eyes and relaxed in the warm surroundings, the flickering flames of the fire releasing my imagination. I allowed myself to dream of following Mallory and Irvine up Everest and my flight of fantasy took me easily past all the known obstacles of the great mountain to the accompaniment of Sibelius' Fifth Symphony. I imagined myself sailing up the north ridge, past the first and second step and to the final pyramid. On, on, on, to the summit itself. "Ah!" I mused. "Mr Blessed Explorer Extraordinaire — the intrepid Everestier!"

Mallory's words on Music and Mountains came to me:

A day spent in the mountains is like some great symphony. Andante, andantissimo sometimes, the first movement — the grim, sickening plod up the moraine, but how forgotten it is when the blue light of dawn flickers over the hard, clear snow! The new motif is ushered in, as it were, very gently on the lesser wind instruments; hautboys and flutes, remote but melodious and infinitely hopeful, caught by the violins in the growing light, and torn out by all the bows with quivering chords as the summits, one by one, are enmeshed in the golden light of day, until at last the whole band, in triumphant accord, has seized the air and romps in magnificent frolic, because there you are at last marching, all a tingle with warm blood, under the sun.

And so throughout the day, successive moods induce the symphonic whole: allegro, while you break the back of the expedition, and the issue is still in doubt; scherzo, perhaps, as you leap up the final rocks of the arête or cut steps in a last short slope, with the ice ships swimming and dancing and bubbling and bounding with magic gaiety over the crisp surface in their mad glissade; and then, for the descent, sometimes again andante, because, while the summit was still to win, you forgot that the business of descending may be serious and long; but in the end, scherzo once more — with the brakes on for the sunset.

Two days later the morning chill hit me, as I slowly crawled out of my tiny tent. Dawn was already breaking. Now young, strong, fit climbers adjusted their bits of equipment and moved expeditiously around the camp.

As I was a little late, I made haste to dress. All went smoothly until I attempted to place my right foot in its boot. The pain was excruciating and I slumped in an embarrassing heap in front of my tent.

Geoff watched me uncomfortably and advised me to take my time. I examined my foot. Forcing the swollen foot into the boot had opened up many of the injuries.

"Oh dear!" I found myself imitating the comedian, Rob Wilton. "If ever a man suffered!"

I applied my trusted techniques, a mixture of oils, powders, cotton wool and large elastoplasts. When at last all was in place, I smothered the foot in vaseline. Slowly, I pushed the object into the boot but, after taking a few steps, I sat down to relieve the pain. Geoff came over to hear my decision. For some time now he had looked forward to climbing Mont Blanc with me.

"I'll be all right," I said. "I've climbed with worse."

Geoff frowned at this. "I think you need your head examined," he said. "But all right then, Mr Blessed. Let's be on our way."

Two hours later, as we left the tree line, the swelling in my foot miraculously subsided, enabling me to keep up, although the pain shot up my leg like exploding electrodes. We were attempting the normal, classic route, via the Gouter Hut at 12,000 feet, then on to the snow fields above to the Vallot Hut, at just over 14,000 feet. And finally, hopefully, along the ridges to the summit at 15,780 feet.

At this point, above the tree line, there is a little railway train, which takes you a mile or so from where you begin climbing the rock. For some reason which is lost to me, Geoff separated from us lower down to make certain arrangements. Now he joined us in a black mood; justifiably, for he had been lumbered with carrying about 120 lbs of metal gear in his rucksack. It is the only time that I have witnessed him do his nut — his wrath was aimed at his unfortunate business partner, who had apparently failed to organise a shareout of the aforementioned gear.

Carrying such a load at 10,000 feet is no joke and we quickly dug into his rucksack, shared out the contents and so remedied the situation. We enjoyed scaling the rocks toward the Gouter Hut and arrived at just over 12,000 feet at about 3 p.m. The hut proved to be warm and spacious and the guardian in charge was a cheerful fellow, with a never-ending supply of steaming soup.

Towards late evening, ever more climbers arrived, until the place was fair busting at the seams, so that when it was time for nighty-nights, it was almost impossible to find a space to lie down. Out of our party of twelve, two decided that this was as high as they wished to go. They had developed bad headaches and bad coughs, with the odd person complaining of toothache.

In the gathering darkness outside, a storm was building up and as the hours passed the full force of it shook the building alarmingly. Geoff's thin face broke into a grin. "Ah, Mr Blessed, it'll blow itself out."

We had been bedded down since 8 p.m., although it is doubtful if anyone actually slept. Time seemed to drag until the guardian suddenly roared loudly, "Mont Blanc!"

This was an order to dress and head for the summit. It was one o'clock and pitch black outside. The wind sounded as strong as ever and chaos reigned in the hut, with everyone clumsily trying to get into their gear. Torches flashed, crampons failed to fit and grunts and curses rent the air.

Miraculously, order finally was achieved and the door

was opened to the full blast of the gale. Snow poured into the hut. *"Allez vous en. Allez vous en,"* roared the guardian.

Adjusting our headlamps, we followed the person in front in a disciplined line out of the hut. Following Geoff through the door, I was thumped by the sudden extreme cold.

Progress was slow initially, as the wind was hitting us head on. It was only when I looked back at the lights in the hut that I appreciated the fact that we were gaining height. To my left, through the driving snow, I could discern the new moon, with Venus sparkling alongside it. It was a thrilling sight and made me realise what a great adventure we had embarked upon, the cold wind, snow and darkness adding to the drama.

Some way above me, on a sharp snow ridge, the beams of the headlamps danced in the blackness. The lights formed a winding trail. Open the pearly gates, I thought, and let the pilgrims in.

After a further twenty minutes, it was sad to see some of these lights turn and descend, defeated by the conditions. The decision to turn back was infectious and more and more people turned away. By the time dawn had broken, half of the contingent of sixty had packed it in.

Mont Blanc is renowned for sudden violent storms and a great many people have lost their lives on the white mountain. It is absolutely imperative for inexperienced climbers to find first-class guides when attempting these Alpine giants, and totally to respect their judgement. As other guides instructed their clients to return to the Gouter Hut, Geoff, thank God, decided that the conditions were acceptable and that we were fit enough to continue.

This decision cheered us enormously. In appearance I bore some similarity to Scott of the Antarctic; my beard was frozen solid, icicles hung down almost to my chest. On one occasion I foolishly removed my outer glove to adjust one of my crampons. This rendered my left hand useless for about twenty minutes and I used every means to warm it again and to stimulate circulation. Geoff admonished me with a shake of his head and we ploughed on.

Higher and higher and higher we climbed. The snow had now stopped but the wind persisted; even with first class wind-proof clothing it seemed able to penetrate to every part of the body. The climbing party in front of us suddenly came to an abrupt halt: immediately in front of them was a huge, yawning chasm, which was partly concealed by a treacherous covering of snow. The Swiss guide's group looked distinctly despondent, recoiling in horror at the prospect of trying to cross it.

A quick decision was made and they too turned in their tracks and made for the warmth of the Gouter Hut. We now appreciated the experience we had gained on La Mer de Glace two days before. This crevasse was no more intimidating than the ones we had encountered there. Nevertheless, we were nonplussed as to how to tackle it.

Geoff's moment had come. Employing great judgement and dexterity, he successfully navigated a way over. Half an hour later the rest of us joined him and we were as proud as punch, as we were now the only climbing party left. The terrain before us now levelled off as we approached the Vallot Hut at 14,000 feet. The snow was deceptively deep, forcing us to stop repeatedly to regain our breath. We were also beginning to tire, as the altitude started to take effect.

The half mile to the hut took forever. The damned wind was murderous and the early morning sun made no appreciable difference to temperature. But, at last we made it. What a contrast to the Gouter Hut! Instead of the warm wood of the other building, this was made of metal and absolutely freezing, but at least it kept out the infernal wind. We looked a poor lot, our ice encrusted bodies bent over in pain and tiredness.

Geoff pointed to the window and the high snow ridge leading on and on to the summit of Mont Blanc. "You can see the objective clear enough," he said.

I had been so intent on reaching the hut that I hadn't realised that our goal was so near. In spite of the bad conditions, I was as happy as a sand boy at having reached over 14,000 feet for the first time in my life.

We all agreed to a fifteen minute rest. Four of the lads felt they couldn't go a step further; the altitude and vicious wind and paralysing headaches had brought them to a standstill. One stocky fellow with blonde hair wept with frustration but wished the rest of us the best. He was a school teacher, a gutsy, cheerful man, with whom I had developed a happy rapport. I did everything in my power to persuade him to go for the summit but he smiled, saying, "I'm happy with 14,000 feet, Brian."

Sitting huddled with my coffee, my thoughts turned

to Mallory. The great climber in his time climbed Mont Blanc twice:

> Is not an ascent of Mont Blanc under any circumstances supremely satisfying? Or is it merely a hymn of praise to my mistress? I confess I have never walked up to the summit from the Grand Mulet; but I should be far from despising such an enterprise. A great mountain is always greater than we know; it has mysteries, surprises, hidden purposes, it holds always something in store for us. One need not go far to learn that Mont Blanc is capable *de tout*. It has greatness beyond our guessing — genius if you like — that indefinable something about a mountain, to which we know but one response: The spirit of adventure.

We now moved upwards, the fatigue of the last few hours seeming to evaporate. The five remaining climbers moved rhythmically and in unison, held together by a strong rope, like an umbilical cord. If one of us weakened, the others cheerfully encouraged him to go on. At last the sun began to warm the air and helped our progress, energising tired limbs.

Two hundred yards to go. Over on the right we observed the shattered remains of a small aircraft that had crashed into the side of the ridge. Gradually, ever so gradually, the summit came into view. A few more steps and we were there, at 15,782 feet high.

Each man embraced the other and emotions ran high. The sky was vibrant blue and free of cloud. Even our old enemy, the wind, had subsided. It was now nine o'clock and we had been climbing for eight hours. The view in every direction was glorious; the summit has a large flat top and we moved about, naming the scores of peaks below us.

My head hummed with the excitement of it all. I sat down and relaxed. All was lovely and we were at peace with the world. Again, my thoughts turned to Mallory and, with Geoff beside me, tried to remember his description of his ascent of Mont Blanc. I spoke incoherently, making little sense, but here are the actual words Mallory wrote:

A breeze cool and bracing seemed to gather force as they plodded up the long slopes, more gentle now as they approached the final goal. He felt the wind about him with its old, strange music. His thought became less conscious, less continuous. Rather than thinking or feeling, he was simply listening — listening for distant voices, scarcely articulate . . .

The solemn dome resting on those marvellous buttresses, fine and firm above all its chasms of ice, its towers and crags; a place where desires point and aspirations end; very, very high and lovely, long suffering and wise . . . experience, slowly and wonderfully filtered; at last a purged remainder . . . And what is that? What more than the infinite knowledge that is all worthwhile — all one strives for? . . . How to get the best of all? One must conquer, achieve, get to the top; one must know the

end to be convinced that one can win the end —
to know there's no dream that mustn't be dared
. . . Is this the summit, crowning the day? How
cool and quiet! We're not exultant; but delightful,
joyful, soberly astonished . . . Have we vanquished
the enemy? None but ourselves . . . Have we won
the kingdom? No . . . and yes. We have achieved
the ultimate satisfaction . . . fulfilled the destiny
. . . to struggle and to understand — never this
last without the other, such is the law . . . We've
only been obeying the old law then? Ah! But it's
THE law . . . And we understand a little more . . .

During our descent, we stopped for the briefest of
stays at the Gouter Hut, refreshing ourselves with bowls
of soup before speeding off impatiently for Chamonix.
In climbing circles it is understood that once you have
attained the summit, you must make haste down to the
safer regions. On this occasion, we were aided by pieces
of flat wood, which we placed underneath our backsides,
enabling us to toboggan down the gentle ice fields at
the speed of light. This mode of transport was much
welcomed by Yours Truly, as my foot was in a frightful
state, with blood pouring freely from the wounds and
turning my beige coloured socks into dark vermilion!
Back with Breda and her family that evening by the
warm fire, my eyes fixed firmly on the distinctive shape
of the mighty, white mountain. Its towers, crags, dome
and glaciers vibrated in the haunting light of the moon.
Geoff sat beside me, ruffled my hair, and whispered in
my ear, "Climbed it, eh, Mr Blessed? Climbed it!"

From that day, I vowed to go to Everest one day, to follow in the footsteps of Mallory and Irvine and their magnificent companions and to tell their story. Did not Mallory say, "To know there's no dream that mustn't be dared . . ."

"Right then!" I thought. "I'm going to have a go!"

Brave words indeed but, as my theatrical agent always says, "Words cost nothing."

CHAPTER
FIVE

The Horse of the Year Show

In the autumn each year, it is time for the Horse of the Year Show at Olympia in London. The equestrian world, in response to the clarion call of Raymond Brookes-Ward, pricks up its ears, tosses its mane and with unbridled joy trots, canters and gallops apace towards the sacred portals that house the arena of bounding delight.

Yes indeed! My goodness me! How popular the show is. With a devotion that surpasses the monks of Athos, families from far and wide flock to that much loved venue and pay homage to the fine horses and riders within. Adoring children entreat tolerant parents to allow them to stay up late and watch TV in the hope that they will see their special favourite clear the last fence and win the day. Throughout the land the silver screen bursts into life with Mozart's cheerful Rondo from *A Musical Joke*, calling all humans with centaur tendencies to drop their daily duties and join the rest of the nation in equine bliss.

During this week of hay-nets, coarse mix, pony

nuts, oats, bran, saddle soap and hoof-oil, my home in Surrey used to reverberate to the sound of groans, moans and breathless ecstasy, as each competitor failed or succeeded in turn. My small daughter and her cronies caught the fever and proudly showed me their enchanting "My Little Pony" toys. What a glittering array they were, with colours of every description. In hidden dens, round corners, under tables and discreetly tucked away into higgledy-piggledy ingle-nooks, I espied infant owners with delicate fingers adjusting minuscule bridles and applying pink, yellow and white brushes and combs to soft long manes of corresponding or contrasting colour.

A pretty dark-haired, round-faced girl of eight called Heather gave me a nod of approval and allowed me to share the space of her inner sanctum. In the quiet, as the last stroke was applied to the white mane, her tiny far away voice cooed to me, "Hush now, please, hush!" In that timeless moment, as the universe itself became still, she lowered her head and became one with her steed, planting upon it a kiss of purity and light.

Up the stairs I trundled with the frolic of children's ditties ringing in my ears: "Horsey, horsey, don't you stop, just let your feet go clippety-clop, your tail goes swish and the wheels go round. Giddy up, we're homeward bound . . ."

Back to the television, where Raymond Brookes-Ward's unmistakable, resonant voice and David Vine's familiar face and cosy manner made me feel part of the continuing drama. I was not alone. Frenzied adults had difficulty keeping their seats as the excitement mounted.

"Oh no!" "Oh yes!" They shouted by turns.

"He's knocked down the last fence! I don't believe it!"

"Graham Fletcher always does that!"

"Oh, Tauna Dora is such a good horse!"

"Yes!" emoted a red-haired lady from Woking. "And he's so adorable! He looks positively ravishing on Buttevant Boy!"

Horse after horse cantered, snorted, jumped and refused before our fascinated eyes. The redoubtable Paddy McMahon, on the much-loved Penwood Forge Mill, had for years gladdened our hearts on winter evenings. The combination of Anne Moore and her horse, Psalm, had also satisfied the senses and lifted the hearts of an adoring public. That great character Ted Edgar steamed ahead with bristling reins, as his rampant steed Uncle Max galloped as if there were no tomorrow, taking fences, walls and anything in his path and only relenting when on the point of extinction.

David Broome wowed the critics with his graceful style, and Eddie Macken on Boomerang rubbed shoulders with greatness and challenged him to the narrowness of a tenth of a second. As John Wayne so aptly said in the western *El Dorado*, "I wouldn't want to live on the difference." Last, but by no means least, there was Harvey Smith. In riding circles, heads nodded and grudgingly conceded that Harvey was second to none in judging horse flesh.

When it came to horsemanship, however, this sceptred isle did not have it all its own way. From over the seas appeared Siegfried, eager to conquer all. "Beware of the

Hun in the sun." Out of that solar orb also appeared Alvin Schockemohle on his white horse (sorry, sorry! — grey horse), and the glittering prizes, one by one, came his way. So effortless and smooth was his riding, that horse and rider appeared as one. It was as if one were looking back in history at Charon, the centaur teacher of Hercules in ancient Greece.

He must make a mistake, we thought. All that was needed was for him to sneeze and then he might just tickle a fence. Could not someone sprinkle the sawdust with a little pepper? No! No! Shame on such thoughts. Alvin and his steed won and won and we looked on in wonder. Nowhere in Britain could a combination be found to challenge the German duo. To top it all, damn it, he was a thoroughly nice man and helpful and kind to all. Even David Broome, with the camera focused closely on his eyes, admitted that he was one of the nicest men he'd ever met. But once upon a time, my concerned reader, over the hills and far away in the village of Compton Dando, there was a horse to strike terror into the hearts of all who beheld him. A mighty white horse (sorry, grey) by the name of Klaus. German by name but British from muzzle to tail. And who had been chosen to ride this fiery steed? Why none other than Yours Truly, the Mighty Toad himself — Brian Blessed!

In 1973, I was invited to the Horse of the Year Show to take part in a charity event. It was to be a light-hearted competition featuring several teams, each composed of a jockey, an equestrian and a personality from the entertainment world. It was to take place on a Friday evening, a few hours before the big guns competed for the major honours.

My riding history wasn't too bad. It had started seven years before, when I was cast as Porthos in the BBC production of *The Three Musketeers*, with my dear colleague, Jeremy Brett, playing the dashing D'Artagnan. It proved to be a great romp and I enjoyed myself enormously. It was my first experience of horses and I was given a good grounding in basic technique by an outstanding rider called Billy Walsh. Billy owned a vast complex of stables alongside Richmond Park and employed a small army of grooms and stable staff to look after his fine ponies. The comedian Jimmy Edwards stabled his large polo pony there. The much loved actor and singer David Healy was married to Billy's daughter and, being a fine rider, assisted in our tuition.

The Sunday rides were particularly exciting, with a large group of around forty horses trotting and cantering over the undulating grounds of the park. We were a mixed bunch comprising ex-army officers, thespians, policemen, businessmen and professional polo players. On one occasion, we lined up like the Charge of the Light Brigade and a Major, who I thought was as pissed as a newt roared out "Charge!" No doubt he was reliving some event from his past and we all set off at a tremendous gallop, clearing ditches and hedges and having a whale of a time.

A teacher called Colonel Smolski, whom I had met when first seeking lessons, had stables nearby. He now hated my guts, as I had selected his rival as my tutor, and he shouted from some nearby trees, "Brian Blessed, you ride like a flat fart!"

Gradually, through David's guidance, I managed to feel comfortable and natural on horseback. Years passed and my riding improved somewhat. Film companies would actually cast me partly because of my confidence on a horse. A most rewarding experience was riding bare-back, when playing a character called Talthybius in the film of the *Trojan Women*, which was shot on location in Spain. My horse was a white horse (sorry, grey) called Bacchus, who had a beautiful mane. I looked after him myself for five months. Terrific experience!

During this time I was doubly fortunate to meet a mysterious Moor called Mahmood, who was in charge of the hundreds of riders who made up the ancient Greek army in the film. Some of these fierce riders belonged to a remote tribe, who lived in the Atlas Mountains and were known as the Blue Riders. Their bodies were blue because the dye in their clothes ran when they perspired and stained their skin. Mahmood said they were the best riders in the world, as they could gallop bare-back at breakneck speed and yet pull up on a sixpence. I joined them once or twice but found the exercise quite beyond me.

Therefore, my dears, when I arrived that Friday night at Olympia, I was game for anything! At the time I was filming a serial for Yorkshire Television called *The Boy Dominic*, so officially I was riding for them. A goodly crowd of spectators had gathered around the arena and the BBC camera crews were busy inspecting their equipment.

Actors and actresses were much in evidence and taking it all very seriously. They were all dressed immaculately in black polished riding boots, jackets and breeches and fine well-fitting hats. Oh dear! I thought, this isn't my scene at all. This was supposed to be a bit of fun, like pass the parcel, except, of course, we were passing the baton.

My eyes searched desperately for the likes of Jimmy Edwards or Harry Secombe, as these were the kind of personalities that I had been expecting. Great Heavens! I felt as if I was competing for Olympic Gold! To say I looked the odd man out is the understatement of the century. I had arrived in my comfortable scruffy·brown corduroy jacket and baggy trousers. Though they were clean, I often used them for gardening. In any case I didn't possess any riding gear. Devil take it! I didn't give a damn.

The officials were none too pleased with my apparel, and they insisted that I wear a riding hat. It was several sizes too small but, with much pressing and pulling, it finally adhered to my head. Yorkshire Television then introduced me to my horse, the aforementioned Klaus. He was a huge horse of the type that Watneys use when advertising their breweries. Big Klaus took my breath away.

"Excuse me," I enquired. "I think he's absolutely wonderful but can he jump four-foot fences?"

My Yorkshire friends frowned indignantly and replied shortly, "Of course he can. He's as strong as a bull!"

"I don't doubt that," I replied, "but I do doubt he can jump!"

A young fellow mounted him and trundled towards one of the exercise fences. There Klaus dug his feet in and screamed! I mean screamed! I've never heard a horse scream like that. He sounded like a female rhinoceros in labour! I kissed the poor lamb, stroked his neck and waved goodbye, as they led him back to the stables for a soothing bran-mash to calm his shattered nerves.

Now I was without a mount. As I walked back to the arena to watch the other thespians at work, I saw Gerald Harper of *Hadleigh* fame and the equally popular Robert Hardy looking resplendent on their respective mounts. They waved a friendly hello and painstakingly steered their horses around the practice fences.

I fastened my gaze on Gerald's horse. He, too, was representing Yorkshire Television and he was a big lad and perfectly capable of carrying me — the horse, I mean, not Gerald.

"Couldn't I ride Gerald's horse, when Gerald has had his turn in the competition?" I enquired.

The officials raised no objection and Gerald generously acquiesced. Five minutes later he rode up to me and informed me that it wasn't now possible for me to use his horse, as he had been asked to ride twice. Apparently, some actor had failed to turn up, and Gerald would be filling the vacancy. Considering my size, he said, it would not be fair to ask the horse to carry me round as well. I was once again without a mount.

At that moment, the actress Caroline Mortimer took a terrible tumble from her horse, whilst jumping a fence.

"Look," I said to worried officials, "it doesn't matter. When the equestrian in my team jumps her round and hands the baton to me, I'll vault over the fences myself and then hand the baton to the jockey." This suggestion confused the officials but after much deliberation, they grudgingly agreed and the die was cast.

Now I was introduced to the lady equestrian in question. She was dark-haired, pretty and thin as a matchstick. She was so tense and bottled up that she moved continuously on the spot, reminding me of Warwick the Third. I cannot for the life of me remember her name, but it was definitely double barrelled — rather like the name of a lady I once knew called Fulvia Fortesque Fulworthy Leeston-Smith. So, if you will forgive me, I will apply this name to her. I remember her horse's name clearly. It was Chocolate Way Misselfore!

We shook hands politely and she gave me instructions about the baton. "Look, Brian, I will approach you on Chocolate and hand you the baton with my left hand. Do you hear me clearly? My *left* hand. And you will take it with your *right* hand."

I thanked her for her meticulous instructions and shook hands with Jack Midge, the jockey, who smiled wistfully and whispered in my ear, "What a fandango about nothing! Just enjoy yourself, Brian. See you later."

I had a chat with Robert Hardy, a chum I'd known on and off for years. He was very proud that he had brought his own horse to the show. It was a mare and she was a beauty, plaits and all. They made a handsome couple and

I wished him all the best in the competition. Smashing fella, Robert, and a terrific actor.

I felt a friendly tap on my shoulder and, on turning around, I found myself looking at David Broome.

"Can yer ride?" he enquired.

"Yes," I responded. "I'm okay on a horse."

David smiled and said kindly, "Would you like to ride my Black Watch?"

My mind boggled for a moment (ride a watch? I thought). Then the fog cleared and I realised he meant one of his own great steeds.

"I certainly would. Thank you, David, that's extremely kind of you."

"That's all right," he nodded. "He only requires a little squeeze and a loose rein and he'll find his own way round the course."

From that moment I was the envy of everyone. Black Watch! I ask you! I was thrilled to bits. The news spread quickly and Fulvia in particular was madly excited. In her eyes we were now clear favourites to win. The stage was set and Olympia was packed to capacity. Raymond Brookes-Ward raised the temperature with his rich eloquent voice and battle commenced.

The first equestrian sped round at a goodly pace and smoothly passed the baton to Gerald Harper. The confident thespian moved with alacrity towards the first fence, looking stunningly impressive — and was immediately disqualified!

Gerald froze in his tracks and stared in disbelief. Had all his preparations come to this? And what a ghastly sound the disqualification hooter made! Rather like a cross between the negative noise on *Family Fortunes* and a deep, nasal fart.

"Sorry, old boy," Raymond Brookes-Ward sang out. "I'm afraid you've jumped the last fence first. Bad luck, old chap. Still, ladies and gentlemen, he has another round to come."

Round after round went by with the jockeys and equestrians looking sleek and confident and the thespians looking red-faced and wobbly. There's nothing to beat really, I thought. Their times are slow and we have Black Watch.

The unknown quantity was Robert Hardy. I viewed him suspiciously. His steed was snorting and Robert's face was red and resolute. The sweating equestrian handed him the baton and he was off . . . Off! Off! Off! Right off! Right off course!

He spun round just in time, unlike Gerald, and calmly re-adjusted his seat. He headed slowly, slowly, ever so slowly for the first fence — and stopped. The lady didn't fancy it! He spun round and calmly headed for the first fence again — and stopped. With graceful charm and increased patience, he spun her around once more and slowly, slowly, ever, ever, ever so slowly headed for the last time for the first fence — and stopped. The mare would not move! Gently Robert squeezed his knees and applied the correct pressure. The mare remained as immobile as Lot's wife. Whilst keeping his dignity, Robert brought his strong legs into action, bringing them down with disciplined rhythmic power on the mare's sides. The lady remained impassive.

Throughout this ordeal, Robert had behaved in an

impeccable manner, but even he winced as the hooter bayed out its flatulent wail. All that remained was for the thespian to turn around, move to the exit, and, to the manor born, remove his hat and smile.

Now! By the mast! It was our turn. Fulvia Fortesque Fulworthy Leeston-Smith moved like a bullet. She had the bit between her teeth all right! One fence, two fences, three fences, more . . . the young woman was a delight to watch as she soared over the last fence. The competition was in the bag. With her red face glowing with pride and her eyes wide with excitement, she approached me. Dutifully, as instructed, I put out my right hand to receive it from her left. It was not to be. The gallant equestrian had it in her right hand and, as I re-adjusted, she slammed it in my face. Immediately, my hat, much to my relief, I might say, went ping and shot into the air. At the same moment that great character, Ted Edgar, decided it was time to have some fun and stuck a stick up Black Watch's rear end, which caused him to take to the air. Amidst screams from the crowd, he powered forward with his colossal strength and raced over the first three fences at alarming speed.

On television the arena looks quite spacious. In actual fact it is very small. In next to no time we had reached the far end and Black Watch stopped extremely abruptly. I catapulted over his head and landed on my feet. Instantly I became "Toad the Traffic Queller", "Leader of the Blue Riders". I'd had enough of this poncey competition! I mounted in the flick of an eye, roared Black Watch on, cleared the remaining fences, bounded into the collecting ring where the other competitors were waiting, scattered the lot of them, jumped out again and cleared the terrified TV crews gingerly clinging onto their cameras. I eased my mount back to the stables, tied him up and disappeared into the streets towards Hammersmith and the nearest flicks.

That evening my performance was shown on television as an example of how not to ride. Four days later I received two crates of Irish whiskey from the organisers of the show, in recognition of the "Bravest Ride of the Evening". Black Watch may be as dark as ebony but it did not compare in blackness to the look I received that night from David Broome!

PS: Sorry, Midge.

CHAPTER
SIX

Hats

Over the months back in England, in the cold light
of day, my fervent ambition to climb Everest took a
heavy beating. People smiled, listened sympathetically
and, when they had heard enough, politely excused
themselves and disappeared. My theatrical agent, John
Miller, had breathed a sigh of relief when I returned
from my first Alpine season in one piece. He now had
to try to convince people that I was a dedicated actor
and not a mountaineer. When I look back, I realise what
a pain in the arse I must have been.

John was a rather handsome, tall, thin man of forty
years or more, with a full head of neat, slightly greying
hair and a Clark Gable moustache which highlighted
his smile when he voiced his wicked sense of humour.
He had two children, Mark and Jane, and a pretty
wife named Jean who was sweetness and light itself.
She always listened patiently to my mad ravings about
Mallory and Irvine, while her poor husband busied
himself on the telephone seeking out work for me.

My category in the actors' casting directory, *The
Spotlight*, was "Character/Leading Man", and this label
suited me well. Over the years, I was fortunate enough

to play a variety of roles, always, of course, fitting in a climb whenever possible.

In 1973, during the filming of the series *The Boy Dominic* for Yorkshire Television, I met and fell in love with the renowned and beautiful actress, Hildegard Neil. We were married in Woking, Surrey, and lived in a quaint little abode named Primrose Cottage in Chobham. Our baby daughter, Rosalind, completed our happiness.

Both Hildegard and I share a passionate love of animals, which means we always have a large family of cats and dogs. In fact, the expression "raining cats and dogs" could have been coined to describe us. Every chair in the house is occupied by one of these possessive furries. This "Noah's Ark" way of living was fully demonstrated when visiting friends came face to face with a white Shetland pony, called Misty, eating the dog biscuits in the kitchen!

Throughout this time, I pinned Hildegard's ears back with stories of the early Everest expeditions in the 1920s. At first she found these fascinating, but as time wore on, she found the constant repetition hard to take. She is, by nature, very kind and tolerant, but my obsessive preoccupation with Mallory tested even her great patience to the limit.

Hildegard was willing to meet me half-way, accompanying me to Tunbridge Wells, near which the much loved Harrison's Rocks, High Rocks and Bowles Outdoor Pursuit Centre are situated. With the security of top roping, Hildegard found these climbs, ranging from ten to sixty feet, great fun. Her love of the great outdoors stems from the beaches and beauty spots of Cape Town,

South Africa, where she was born. However, she was never much in evidence on Table Mountain, as the cobras and puff adders inhibited her enjoyment of that beautiful mountain.

On one occasion we spent a day in Swanage, Dorset. The sun shone brightly as we scrambled along the cliffs named Subliminal. We ended the day roped together, doing the tricky traverse across the amphitheatre of rocks. Hildegard surprised me, being totally unconcerned about the vertical exposure. Terrain formed by nature does not worry her unduly; it is man-made structures that give her problems.

On completing the climb, we sat down on the top of the rock face under a small bush, whose shade gave us some relief from the boiling sun. Unfortunately, a large fat adder had the same idea! Hildegard groaned with horror and ran swiftly away, her arms waving dramatically above her head. I, on the other hand, was fascinated by the gorgeous creature. I've always loved snakes and this was a real beauty. It moved gracefully over my boot, as it headed for a cool spot at the base of the bush. Hildegard made an impassioned plea that I leave it alone, maintaining that she had experienced snakes for most of her life in Cape Town and that they should be treated with respect. Therefore, when I eventually joined her unbitten she was greatly relieved.

Months later, when visiting Cape Town to show her parents their new grandchild, I went climbing on Table Mountain. The route I had chosen took me up a fairly easy rock face on Castle Buttress. After an hour or so, I distinctly heard someone shouting for help, in a deep raucous voice. The distressed cry repeated itself every five minutes and seemed to come from a rocky promontory about a hundred yards above me. I shouted, "It's all right. Don't worry, I'm close by. Take it easy!"

My message appeared to do little to calm whoever it was, as the cries for help increased. As always, when alone on the mountains, I had a good rope, pitons, descenders and the like, plus a plentiful supply of food and liquid. After a further, fingery exposed ascent of a narrow groove, I pulled myself up to the safety of a small ledge. Standing on this I had my first view of the distressed caller. It was a huge baboon!

"Jesus!" I exclaimed. "Bloody hell!"

The baboon was accompanied by several other males, all viewing me with surprise. On varying rock ledges in the background, were scores of females and their young. My position was vulnerable, to say the least. Speaking in a soft voice, I enquired how they were keeping, all the while moving imperceptibly away from them. I think they considered me some kind of giant ape and viewed me disdainfully as they moved off, not even giving me the time of day. Later, I was informed that many troops of baboons occupied the mountains and that I should count myself fortunate that I wasn't attacked.

Shortly after, I was offered the part of Augustus Caesar in the BBC series *I Claudius*. This was a terrific offer and it temporarily made me forget George Leigh Mallory. The brilliant adaptation was by Jack Pulman, from the novel by Robert Graves. Herbert Wise, whom I had worked with many years before in *Z Cars*, was the director. The cast was outstanding, featuring Derek Jacobi, Sian Phillips, John Hurt and George Baker amongst others. All in all, it proved to be a wonderful experience, offering every member of the team a tremendous challenge.

Half-way through rehearsals, we had the honour of a visit from Robert Graves, who had come all the way from his home in Majorca. Derek Jacobi, our producer Martin Lisemore and myself were invited to have lunch with him at Television Centre. On that occasion I discovered that Graves had been a close friend of Mallory's. They had even climbed together! Mr Mallory, it seemed, was not prepared to let me forget him for too long.

Graves proved to be a fascinating and gracious man, and his implicit belief that our production of *I Claudius* would be a great success was conveyed with a certainty that transcended ordinary perception. There had been a rather dramatic history of calamity during previous attempts to film it, and many believed it to be accursed. Graves himself admitted that this assertion had a certain credibility, but he maintained with confidence that the curse had been lifted. Claudius, he said, had appeared to him in a dream, and confirmed that the BBC serialisation of the two books would progress without any problems. He added that the sales of the aforementioned books would hit new heights and fill his coffers with much needed cash. His face lit up as he whispered conspiratorially, "The old boy, Claudius, he always looks after me."

Derek Jacobi missed the conversation, as he was on

first call in the studio and his make-up took hours to do. Therefore, Martin and I held the fort, while our esteemed guest continued to fascinate.

He was an elderly man, I believe in his late seventies, but he certainly didn't look it: the smooth skin and shining fair complexion bore the hallmarks of a healthy constitution. Reading between the lines, one deduced that years of coping with financial burdens had kept his mind sharp but his body neglected. Over the last year or so, his mind had thrown away the problems and he had spent a lot of time walking and jogging along his beloved Majorca beaches. His body was now completely rejuvenated.

At one particular moment in the conversation, he stopped mid-stream, his blue-grey eyes staring at some faraway object on the lonely heights of Parnassus. This pause went on for some considerable time, while Martin and I waited for him to rejoin us. It was at this juncture that I introduced the subject of Mallory. Now Graves's eyes took on an intense look, as he expressed surprise at my new line of enquiry.

"Did you know him?" he questioned.

Shaking with laughter, I replied, "No, no. He died before my time, in 1924!"

"Of course he did. Of course he damn well did!" Graves shouted, admonishing himself for his forgetfulness.

"You know, Charles," he continued, "Mallory was wasted at Charterhouse."

I must explain here that Graves was quite convinced that I was Charles Laughton, who had played Claudius in the abortive film version of the 1930s. It would have been impolite of me to correct the great man and, anyway, it was great fun and gave Martin and me endless amusement. The atmosphere was very cordial and Graves displayed the wit and the humour of a man whose evolution was miles ahead of our own.

"Ah, George. Dear George. He was my first friend, you know. Oh yes. And always remained so. Yes, yes, he moved in a world most people didn't understand. Everyone called him Sir Galahad. Ah, George. I did love him so. You had to keep your eyes on him when he led you on a climb or you would be seduced into thinking a pitch was easy because of the ease with which he climbed it.

"Dear Lord! His style, my dear fellow, defied comprehension. Up! Up! Up! He would flow up a rock face in one continuous movement. He had the ability to put his foot high, at the same time bending his shoulder to the knee to propel himself into a gracious curve. Oh my goodness! The whole vision made the heart miss a beat. Such harmony! Such grace! His climbing was like a secret that was quite impossible to fathom.

"He always amused me when he came to a difficult section. He would then attack it with the powerful, controlled insistence of a mongoose wooing a cobra, until at last he had finally mastered it. People said that his movement was cat-like; for me it was more serpentine.

"His elation when he'd climbed a peak was most amusing to observe. On Snowdon one day, drunk with emotion, he hurled stones in the air and shouted in celebration!"

At this point Graves's eyes moistened and slowly closed. After several moments the great man again repeated, "Ah, George. I did love him so!"

It was almost mid-afternoon and Martin and I had to make our goodbyes, as we were needed in the studio. Graves gently shook our hands, wishing us all the best, at the same time asking me to give his kind regards to Alexander Korda, Emlyn Williams and Merle Oberon — he was still quite convinced that I was Charles Laughton! As he departed down the corridor with Martin, he suddenly stopped and turned, and called back to me, "Chartreuse! Green Chartreuse! It sold a lot of copies the first year."

I nodded agreeably, understanding that he was referring to a school magazine that he and the others had compiled with Mallory, at Charterhouse, in 1913.

Then Graves looked at me mischievously and said, "Hats!"

I was completely non-plussed. "Hats?" I replied.

"Yes, hats," Graves continued. "They changed hats, Mallory and Irvine, on the North Col, when they made their final climb on Everest!"

"Why?" I asked.

Graves smiled and remained silent. Then the old boy waved to me and continued on his way. Towards the end of the long corridor, he started to sing "Green Grow The Rushes, Oh", just as he turned out of sight. His pleasant voice echoed back to me, suggesting images of a bygone age.

I quickly followed him down the corridor and repeated my question with increased intensity. "Why did they change hats, Mr Graves?"

He stopped, turned and with a huge grin on his face answered, "Oh, that's festivity!"

CHAPTER
SEVEN

The Ipswich Town Supporter and the Team

During the first week of March 1981, my agent at that time, John Miller, rang to say that Andrew Lloyd Webber and Trevor Nunn wished to see me about a musical they were staging called *Cats*.

"*Cats*!" I replied incredulously. "I couldn't possibly play a cat. There is absolutely nothing feline about me!" Convulsed with laughter, I added, "There really is no point in wasting their time — if it were bears or gorillas, I might possibly be of use. Anyway, John, you know as well as I do, managements putting on musicals these days are looking for rock musicians. I sing 'properly', and anyway I'm completely inexperienced. Let's forget it, John. It's mortifying and a waste of time."

My agent listened patiently but still advised that I should give it a try.

"Give me a little time to think about it," I said and hung up. The thought of going for an interview non-plussed and depressed me.

"What is it?" Hildegard enquired, her grey-green eyes searching my grim countenance.

"Oh, it's another damn musical interview," I groaned. After hearing the basic details, Hildegard suggested we take a walk with the dogs. This is always her technique. It gets me away from distractions such as the telephone and the doorbell. It calms me down and allows me to give vent to whatever is troubling me. Walking across Sunningdale Golf Course, I poured out my frustrations and doubts about the threatened interview.

Every time I had considered a West End musical, it had fizzled out. One such project was a plan to stage *How Green Was My Valley*. The director and producer thought that I was the best thing since sliced bread and maintained that I had just the right quality for the lead. After a week of auditions, they disappeared into thin air.

Other promised roles were King Henry II in a musical of the play *Becket*, and Shylock in a production entitled *Fire Angel*. The management of the latter was adamant that they wanted Shylock to be sung straight, in contrast with Antonio and the rest, who would have the usual rock style of singing. Therefore, they insisted, my voice was perfect for the part. A few days later, they completely changed their minds and decided to have the old Jew also sung in the modern way, which placed it totally outside my range. (All this was before the Italian World Cup, "Nessum Dorma" and Luciano Pavorotti. I find myself indebted, once again, to the BBC for making "serious singers" popular again.)

All these examples I itemised to Hildegard, as we waited for Sunningdale's very own Nick Faldos to make their strokes. She listened with quiet concern and understanding but she was not about to let me get away with it. She felt that to pass up the opportunity to work with people of the calibre of Andrew Lloyd Webber, Trevor Nunn and Gillian Lynne was irresponsible.

Consequently, the next day I found myself outside Andrew Lloyd Webber's flat in London, reluctantly pressing the doorbell. After I had announced myself to the security device, the door buzzed and opened. A sweet young lady introduced herself as Sarah, Andrew's wife, and welcomed me in. "Brian Blessed to see you darling," she projected to another room and disappeared.

For the next forty-five minutes it would be fair to say I was totally flabbergasted by the person in front of me. It was Webber's eyes that first caught the attention — large, brown and penetrating with a suggestion of shyness. His handshake was warm but very quick and to the point, as if the action interfered with his preoccupation, i.e. *Cats*. With movements reminiscent of a Chinese firecracker, he exploded around the room, alighting from time to time on the odd chair, but only for a second. He switched on the stereo system and then followed this almost immediately by playing the piano, all the while talking at the speed of a chipmunk. Various manuscripts and sheets of music hit the air, as he rummaged like Squirrel Nutkin in every corner of the room to find the appropriate song to play me. From time to time he disappeared from the room altogether like a genie.

"Yes, Brian, I'll call you Brian — maybe you like being called Blessed?" Before I could reply he was racing about again. "Yes, Blessed Brian, would you credit it — a friend of mine called Stephen Tate, I discovered the other day, earns his living by decorating — absolute madness! He dances, acts, sings, he does everything wonderfully. He's going to play Growltiger. I think. Yes he is. Yes he is!"

There was a huge pause at this point and I wondered whether the interview was over, or as an audience might say, "Is that the end of the play?" But no. The silence was broken again, as the Chinese firecracker with his head held back observing the ceiling ignited his next bit of blue touch paper.

"Well, well, well, yes, let me see — possibly you would be the cat who sings the last song 'The Ad-Dressing of Cats'. I think Old Deuteronomy will sing it, though that has not been fully decided. Trevor will work that out. Would you like to follow me, Blessed, on the piano? Doesn't matter that you can't read music. No one can these days."

The love and enthusiasm he displayed for his project rendered him pretty well incoherent as the words tumbled out. "This song is about Mungojerrie and Rumpleteazer, sweet lovable little cats, petty thieves, yes, yes, oh yes, that's what they are, engaging rogues, they, ah yes! They pinch anything. Mungojerrie rather eggs Rumpleteazer on, I'm afraid. Tut, tut, tut!"

Webber then fired off a series of short laughs, catching his breath each time, as if he were having trouble with his oxygen intake. His excitement knew no bounds and he continued to talk nineteen to the dozen and moved about at the speed of light.

"Mungojerrie and Rumpleteazer, yes yes, yes. Of course you are not really suited for either part, as you would need to be able to dance. Of course you can't dance — of course, silly of me to mention it! Possibly, possibly, let me see."

During the next five minutes he rapped out the names of numerous felines — Skimbleshanks the Railway Cat, Munkustrap, Macavity, Gus, Bustopher Jones, Quaxo — accompanying each character he mentioned with their own special tune. The music sounded exciting and original and one piece in particular struck me as moving and mystical. It related to Old Deuteronomy.

"This could suit you — yes, yes, indeed," he shouted.

My heart skipped a beat at the prospect of singing it. Then he dismissed the idea with a shrug. "No, no, no, I'm forgetting, Blessed, Deuteronomy doesn't sing it, other cats do. Wouldn't suit you at all. Here's a snippet from the Jellicle Ball."

Jellicle cats come out tonight,
Jellicle cats come one, come all.

"Do you like it?" he grinned.

"Yes," I nodded, breathlessly.

"I'm afraid that's not for you either, Blessed," he said shaking his head. "No, no, no, where do I fit you in? Possibly, possibly Growltiger, who starts as the Theatre Cat and becomes a pirate. Maybe that's the one for you — yes, of course, yes." Immediately his hands manipulated the chords of the piano again, as he played Growltiger's song, "Billy McCaw".

"No, no, silly me, I don't think so. No, you might need to dance for that one, too. Oh dear, oh dear."

For a second he was still and I almost felt compelled to look for the key in his back to wind him up again. The thought was unnecessary, as he erupted into life again.

"Would you believe it, Blessed — er sorry, er Brian, — someone told me the other day that the great Chaliapin himself couldn't read music. Anyway, try singing 'The Ad-Dressing of Cats', which is the last song of the musical."

I launched myself into it and found the tune fairly easy to follow and great fun.

"Good heavens, Blessed — er sorry, Brian — yes, you have an amazing range. Yes, possibly the last note could be a B flat or a top C. All right with you?"

"Certainly," I replied, enjoying watching his eyes grow larger. For the first time in my life, since leaving primary school, I was enjoying singing.

"Good, good, good." He continued describing scenes and sounds and turned on the stereo again to play Paul Nicholas singing "Magical Mr Mistoffolees". The crescendo of music combined with his increasingly emotional deliberations on the musical made my head spin.

"Andrew," I addressed him firmly, "I can't understand a word you are saying."

This had a quaint effect on him. He stood still, like a little boy who had lost his lollipop. His white shirt and his short hair clung to him, both soaked with perspiration.

"Yes, quite right," he nodded. "Yes, of course. The

thing is, that — er — er — er — yes, where do I begin? Possibly I could — no, no, that's too confusing. Look, I am doing a musical with Cameron MacKintosh — lovely man, you'll like him, he's so refreshing. At last I've found a man with heart — yes, that's how I would describe him.

"The musical is based on T. S. Eliot's *Old Possum's Book of Practical Cats*. I'm sure Eliot would have approved, as he was a great fan of American musicals. His widow, Valerie Eliot, has given us a great deal of material, his unpublished work, poems, fragments of poems and letters describing future projects. All this convinced Trevor and myself that Eliot was going to write a much larger piece about cats. The whole thing is madly exciting, Blessed, with lots of marvellous people. You know Gilly Lynne — you took her up the Matterhorn or something didn't you?"

"No," I replied, "the Ibruzzi mountains."

"Yes, yes, yes," he responded, "something like that. Anyway she is doing the choreography. Hersey, lights; Napier, sets; and, of course, Trevor is directing. I felt a while ago that one unpublished piece was the key to something much greater, that it could have a theatrical life of its own. This is the mysterious core of the musical and I instantly knew that the one person to direct it was Trevor Nunn.

"Trevor wants to see you now at the Fortune Theatre. He will explain all. I don't know where Cameron is. He is supposed to take us over there."

As quickly as she had disappeared, Sarah appeared again, carrying a tray of coffee and smiling broadly, evidently well aware of the bombardment that I had endured. Before I could enter into a conversation with her, Cameron MacKintosh arrived, his face wreathed in smiles. After a quick introduction, we hurried into his black BMW and set off for the theatre.

Thankfully, Webber relaxed in MacKintosh's company and indulged in some jovial teasing. It was quite a surprise to find how young Cameron was. His stillness, engaging smile and easy-going manner put me at ease. However, his air of competence and self-confidence was somewhat undermined when he bashed into a cement bollard turning a corner! On inspecting the damage, Webber said, "Oh, it's nothing, Cameron. Anyway, you've finished with this car. You're taking delivery of a new one tomorrow!"

"Yes," replied the impresario, suitably mollified.

"Well then," continued the song writer, "let's not worry about it. We can leave it here if we have to."

The aspiring star of musicals chipped in, "Well, if you don't want it, fellas, I'll have it!"

"No, you don't, Blessed," Cameron replied, and we drove the dented car to our destination.

Sitting unobtrusively in the darkness of the auditorium, my eyes focused gradually on the cold, dimly lit stage. After making me feel at home, Webber and MacKintosh went about their business. The solitary figure of a man drifted across the stage, played a few notes on the piano and evaporated into the wings, unaware of my presence.

Time went by and the old doubts started to crop up again. I welcomed the cloaking darkness of the auditorium and tried to enjoy the magic of an empty theatre. After a further five minutes, down left of the stage, one of the exit doors opened and a figure, laden with scripts and baggage appeared. After pushing one door back and performing a minor balancing act, the figure felt confident enough to proceed, but was immediately jammed by the returning door. Trying again, undaunted, he managed to squeeze through. It was none other than Trevor Nunn!

Casting his eyes about and satisfying himself that he was alone, he pulled a flask from his bag and drank some coffee. I sank deeply into my seat and was able to observe him unnoticed.

He was relaxing and I made no attempt to interrupt him. My mind sailed back to an autumn night in 1963 when I lived in Ormond House Cottage, in Richmond, Surrey. On that evening, I was watching a BBC sports programme about that magnificent British heavyweight boxer, Henry Cooper, when the doorbell rang. I answered it and was engulfed by an army of thespians, spearheaded by my actress friend, Susan Engel. It had been several years since I had seen her and she was a welcome sight.

Susan is a strikingly handsome, tall lady and she held me in a great bear hug as her friends swept past me, filling every cranny of my small cottage.

"You ugly creep," she roared. "You untalented, smelly, retarded, unsociable, filthy, pox-ridden, flat-footed Barnsley bastard!"

We laughed happily together, as she covered my face in kisses.

"These are my friends," she emoted. "And they're all bloody marvellous and wonderfully talented!"

"Hello, Brian, nice to meet you." Greetings were soon accompanied by lots of willing hands assisting me at record speed to pour out the drinks. It was the start of a raucous evening in which imagination soared and passionate debate took wing.

My guests were the nucleus of the Royal Shakespeare Theatre Company, young, divine people, their hearts and minds throbbing with excitement at the prospect of embracing the unlimited vistas of "The Bard". Their openness about their aspirations encouraged me to contribute my own wilder ideas and pet theories about this and that.

The evening swept on and it was noticeable that one gentleman, boxed into a corner by the door, kept a distinctly low profile. My eyes focused on him and I homed in, making my way through the intervening bodies to sit by his side. He smiled gently and proffered his hand.

"Trevor Nunn. Pleased to meet you, Brian."

"Pleased to meet you," I nodded.

His eyes scanned the chaos in the room. "I'm afraid that we've rather taken over your home. Please feel free to boot us out whenever you like."

He seemed gentle but assured, with a reserve that suggested a quiet self-confidence. His eyes had a strange, oriental quality. His black hair and dark short beard accentuated the pallor of his complexion but his smile was warm and effortless; a graceful man. But the most remarkable thing about him was that he was wearing a blue football shirt.

"Do you follow some team, Trevor?" I twinkled.

"Yes, I'm an Ipswich Town supporter . . ."

Well, that was it. For the next hour we were two little boys, enthusing about our favourite subject — not Shakespeare, but football! Ipswich players like Crawford and Phillips, managers such as Ramsey and Robson. Trevor's eyes danced and his chest swelled with pride at the thought of his beloved boys in blue.

Over the years that followed, we would sometimes come into contact at film premieres or parties and always we picked up where we had left off — with every aspect of Ipswich Town Football Club. But we never actually worked together.

Ever so gradually, I returned to the present and the auditorium of the Fortune Theatre, as I watched Trevor munching sandwiches.

"Come and say hello." It was Webber standing by my side. "I think, Blessed, that Trevor's going to be a little bit tired. He's just finished filming one of those heavy Russian pieces, *The Three Sisters*."

There was no doubt at all that when Trevor saw me, he was totally astonished.

"Hello, Brian!" he said. "What are you doing here?"

"Well," I replied. "Andrew Lloyd Webber says that you want to see me about his musical."

As I said this, Webber disappeared again. Trevor put a kindly arm round me and confessed that he knew nothing about it.

"Come and sit down," he continued. "Would you like a drink of coffee?"

I nodded and he poured me a cup from his flask. His face broke into a smile, as he said ever so gently, "This is not for you, is it love?"

"I couldn't agree more, Trevor."

"Can you sing, Brian?"

"Actually, I can," I smiled.

"Well, be my guest. Have a go?"

I climbed onto the stage and sang "God Save The Queen" to warm up. Then I moved on to the powerful opening tenor aria from *Aida*. This made Webber, who had appeared again, hit the sides of the walls of the auditorium with his hands. I didn't know whether it was because my voice was offending or pleasing him. I had to perform without any accompaniment and when I'd finished, Trevor came forward.

"Where have you been hiding this all these years? Look, I'll talk to you tomorrow. I have a great many people to meet but I'm delighted you've come."

With that, I made my way backstage and walked smack into the familiar face of Stephen Tate. He was falling about with laughter and in a cod Yorkshire accent said, "By Gum, Lad! I'll bet tha felt reet bloody silly!"

"Tha's bloody reet," I replied. "God knows what I'm doing here! What's it all about?"

Stephen looked me up and down and, trying not to laugh, he said, "It was an audition, Brian! God himself would have to audition for a Lloyd Webber musical. They're holding auditions."

He pointed to a small side door, which opened onto

the narrow corridor that led to the street. To my utter astonishment, it was crammed full of people, awaiting their turn to go on. I had quite simply failed to grasp the fact that this was audition time.

"Why don't you stick around for a few minutes and watch," Stephen suggested. "It'll be an eye-opener for you. The world of musicals is a totally different ball game from the one you're used to."

And so it proved. I watched old and young alike sing, dance and perform gymnastics. The last image of the day was a man imitating Elvis Presley singing "Blue Suede Shoes".

The following morning, Hildegard called me to the phone. It was John, my agent.

"Brian, do you have a good supply of leg warmers? And how's your form on blocks, these days?"

"What?"

"Well, they've offered you one of the leads in *Cats*. They're not sure yet which part it will be, but Cameron says trust him and all will be well."

Hildegard was delighted. After all these years, at last I was going to sing! Her enthusiasm was infectious and before long I was jogging vigorously with our dogs across Chobham Common, pouring with sweat and whistling periodically to make sure the odd straggling canine kept up with me.

My thoughts turned to the prospect of the new project ahead. I had witnessed the extraordinary talent of Gillian Lynne on the film *Man Of La Mancha*. Over the ensuing months her talent would receive world-wide recognition. Webber was already world famous. What a privilege to be going to sing his music. John Napier was to design our show and David Hersey to light it. Both men were the unrivalled leaders in their fields and I had many a time witnessed their classy work.

As for Trevor Nunn, how does one begin to evaluate a director of his calibre? His record speaks for itself: twenty-five years or more of service to Shakespeare, both at Stratford and in London, electrifying audiences with his vast canon of productions. His self-effacing, unassuming manner, masks a visionary mind that is always searching and learning. But it is the regard his actors have for him that is the most revealing.

To a woman and a man, they like and love him unreservedly. On the first day of rehearsals for *Cats* in Chiswick, in response to my enquiry about him, Judi Dench replied, "If he asked me to lie down in front of a double-decker bus, I would do it."

Standing on top of the highest hill on Chobham Common, where people fly their model aircraft, I shook with excitement and felt like flying myself.

And so to that first day. It was truly fascinating, with the Chinese firecracker playing the piano. He switched on the vast stereo systems to play Paul Nicholas singing "Old Deuteronomy" and "Mr Mistoffelees", both numbers having been recorded earlier.

Speaking clearly and precisely, his eyes embracing us all, Trevor painstakingly described the basic story line. The gist of it was that each year in the middle of a large rubbish tip, a number of alley cats perform an entertainment called the Jellicle Ball. Wise Old Deuteronomy, the revered guest cat, will choose one

114

of these felines, just before dawn, to go to the Heaviside Layer, which is higher than the Russell Hotel, and be born again. The only cat that does not participate is Bustopher Jones, the cat about town, who simply passes through.

My story line is abridged and short. In actual fact Trevor, Andrew and Gilly expounded at great length on their ideas and talked that entire first day. They went on for half of the next day as well. The cast smiled, laughed and stared incredulously as the Big Three entertained us royally.

"The holiday is over," Trevor said smilingly. "Now it's your turn. Introduce yourselves."

Sitting in a circle, we all identified ourselves. It was good to see that Stephen Tate had made it, and with smiles and winks he made me feel a little more at ease. The cast would have to dance till they dropped, I gathered. Mercifully, Judi Dench and I were exempt.

Judi observed, "Wayne Sleep can tie his body in knots."

I replied, "I'm still at a loss to know which part I'm playing. It's obvious that you will play Grizabella. Maybe I'm the chorus, telling the story or something."

I found myself surrounded by a bevy of beautiful, curvacious young ladies, introducing themselves. They were all stunningly fit and their youthful features and bright eyes flashed with vitality.

"I'm Sharon Lee-Hill," said one, her bright leotard falling from her shoulders, as she started to dress in front of me. "I loved you in *Flash Gordon*."

"Thank you," I replied.

"I'm Bonnie Langford," said a thin, petite lady.

Names from every direction: Geraldine Gardner, Femi Taylor, Sarah Brightman, Myra Sands. Lovely ladies, everywhere. The room echoed with their shouts.

"It's all right," called Susan Jane Tanner. "None of us knows what we are playing. All will be revealed in time."

A resonant male voice sounded in my ear: "I'd keep very quiet about the fact that you can't dance, Brian. It's obviously something Andrew overlooked. Just float around and we'll cover you." As he finished speaking, he smiled broadly and covered up like a boxer on the ropes. "Not the face, Brian, not the face!" Then he introduced himself as Jeff Shankley.

"Right! Leave Golly alone!" Gilly grinned, clearly pleased that some company spirit was being born. My nickname, Golly, had been invented by her all those years ago in Rome and was quickly adopted by all and sundry.

We sat on the wooden floor of the large rehearsal room and awaited our first instructions. After telling us of her great faith in the musical and her confidence in the assembled cast, Gilly changed gear and laid down the law in no uncertain terms.

"For the next six weeks, you will be worked to a standstill. We are assaying a piece which makes unremitting demands; a non-stop singing, non-stop dancing musical from its first chord to its last. To attain the fluidity of motion that is so characteristic of cats, you will be called on to stretch yourselves far beyond your usual standards. Quite simply, from this moment on, you must devote all your time and energy to thinking and feeling and behaving like cats. If you are to get anywhere near the standard that Trevor, Andrew and I will demand, you must employ absolute discipline. You're all grown-ups, so I don't want to sound like a schoolteacher, but I do recommend that you cut down on parties and don't stay up late. Tiredness can cause injuries and effect your vocal chords.

"Now, I'm going to stop for a fifteen-minute coffee break. Then I want you back in here for our first session."

"What do Judi and I do?" I enquired.

Gilly smiled and advised us to do as many of the movements as we could and then carry on with exercises with which we felt at home.

As an actor, I frequently played barons, kings or pirates leading my men into battle. This had developed to such an extent, that I had virtually forgotten what it was like to work with the fair sex. To suddenly find myself confronted with scores of casual, pretty ladies with legs wide open and toes pointing to the North and South, was a little disconcerting. They had an air of relaxation and unselfconsciousness I found very refreshing.

My participation in the dance exercises sometimes proved to be counter-productive, as my heavy muscle-bound frame, from years of judo and weights, was unreceptive to Gilly's entreaties. "Come on, Golly! Come on. Bend a bit more! That's it. No! Don't fall over!"

In response to her instructions, I would mutter under

my breath, "Bollocks to this! I feel a right bloody nancy!"

On one such occasion, the pretty young lady in front of me, Finola Hughes, started giggling and lost her balance.

"God, Gilly! How am I supposed to twist and bend like that? I can't possibly move my shoulders like Kenn Wells. He's the Indian Rubber man. This is worse than being asked to be a tulip at drama school. I'm going to do myself a mischief, I could end up singing falsetto!"

Gilly recommended some new exercises which, she said, might do wonders for my sex life. By this time everyone was in stitches and serious work had ground to a complete halt.

When rehearsals were working smoothly, it was really quite moving to watch twenty-five or so dedicated young people, making concentrated efforts to achieve what was expected of them by their inspirational teacher. Gilly drove them mercilessly but always applied the brakes when necessary and invested all rehearsals with humour and relaxation.

There were days when the rehearsal room positively shook. Bodies, glistening with sweat, pounded the floor. Arms twirled, chests heaved, stomach muscles tensed and legs propelled feet in all directions. I would exercise alongside the others with my mixture of leg-bends, stomach pulls and press-ups. Gilly, at the front, reminiscent of Eve in the Garden of Eden, with just a suggestion of material to hide her private parts, performed every exercise with them with consummate ease and shouted instructions at the same time equally effortlessly.

Gradually, by dint of this blazing effort, the cast seemed to me to move with the power and rhythm of waves in the ocean to the sound of Lindsey Dolan on the piano. Their eyes were feverishly aware of their fellow artists and it became plain that we were in accord and becoming a team. We lay on the floor and, as the heavy breathing subsided, Gilly said softly, "Tense the face — and relax. Now the mouth — and relax. Now the eyes — and relax . . ." The floor was a cloud and we sank gently through it to sleep a short, deep sleep. Trevor Nunn had shared this experience from a balcony above and he nodded and smiled his approval.

Next it was over to Tony Stenson, the deputy conductor, as we transferred our attention to singing. Tape recorders emerged from handbags, briefcases and shopping baskets, to record the songs and music that we were being taught. "Basses, baritones, to the left," Tony directed us. "Tenors to the right, please. Sopranos, altos here. Have you got enough room? Come and sit on my chair. Right then, you lovely people. We'll start with the 'Naming of Cats'."

We spoke the opening line in unison.

> The naming of cats is a difficult matter,
> It isn't just one of your holiday games.

Under the watchful eyes of David Firman, the musical director, and David Cullen, who was responsible for the orchestration, the music started to sink in and take shape.

It was confirmed that I would play Old Deuteronomy and sing the last song in the show, "The Ad-Dressing of Cats". It was a song with quite a range and great fun to sing, under the watchful ear and splendid tuition of Tony Stenson.

Myriads of smaller rehearsal rooms surrounded the main hall, each occupied by singers belting out their songs and filling the air with a cacophony of sound. In a rare moment of silence, I discerned in the distance Judi Dench singing a haunting song called "Memory". On descending the stairs I came face to face with a surprisingly quiet Andrew Lloyd Webber, who enquired gently if I could learn a short song to start Act Two, entitled "The Moments of Happiness".

"Delighted, Andrew," was my response. I have always loved the lyrics of this little snippet of music, Eliot at his mystical and esoteric best.

The basic shape of the musical began to emerge as Trevor started to make his formidable presence felt. We always waited with bated breath for him to speak and then hung on his every word.

Laying down his black coffee, he gave us examples of T. S. Eliot's original mind and stated quietly that he would have given up his entire career to have been able to say that he had written "The Naming of Cats". He laid particular emphasis on truth and being. He said that one day science might be able to give tangible proof of the connection between players and audiences. Not for one moment can you fool an audience, he maintained.

He stressed the importance of telling the story, the beginning, middle and end. He smiled broadly and tugged at his small black beard. Then, suddenly in an almost severe mood, he pointed out how daunting was the task of entering the strange world of the cat, laying emphasis on the importance of finding a key to the complex moods of the felines. He gently urged that we be absolutely single-minded in our quest.

For the next two hours, we described cats we had owned or known and then endeavoured to get under their skin and "demonstrate" them. These observations ranged from the comic to the tragic, as we all eagerly and enthusiastically joined in. The session ended with a universal feeling that we had made good progress, owing much to Nunn's great ability to infuse energy and then to guide it methodically onwards. The Ipswich Town Supporter gathered his bag, whispered a faint cheerio and disappeared.

Despite the meticulous warming up process, some few days later, injuries abounded. Gilly's choreography was stunning but devastatingly demanding, and the simple fact was that we were human beings, not cats! One young man to go down, who had endeared himself to me, was Jeff Shankley. He was outstandingly gifted and the thought of losing him horrified us. His cartilage had gone and he was rushed to hospital. John Thornton, who was playing Macavity and who was one of our strongest dancers, was also having trouble. In fact most of the company, in one way or another, were having problems.

The feasibility of mounting the show at all reared its

ugly head, but Cameron MacKintosh just smiled and shrugged his shoulders saying, "It's all going to be fine. Don't worry."

I looked on helplessly. Judi was performing splendidly as she slowly learned how to tap dance for the Gumbie Cat. Then our worst nightmare came true. We heard a sound like a muffled pistol shot and a shriek of pain. Judi's Achilles' tendon had snapped. Everyone descended on her as she collapsed in agony and despair. Picking her up from the wooden floor and placing her on the comfort of a soft chair, I searched for Trevor. He was in the middle of a solo session with Paul Nicholas and, hearing my news, flew like a bird to be at Judi's side. Holding her in his arms, he hugged and kissed her, all the while wiping her eyes and quietly enquiring when the ambulance would arrive. Within half an hour they had both gone, leaving a vacuum behind.

During the next few days the news slowly filtered through that Judi would attempt to play Grizabella but the Gumbie Cat was out of the question. Therefore, Myra Sands, a vivacious clever artist, would play the Gumbie. On the other hand, the news of Jeff Shankley was good, as he seemed to be on the mend and would be back soon.

These incidents had shaken us but the resolve of the company was absolute and we surged on. The show was developing marvellously. Sharon Lee-Hill and Geraldine Gardner were performing the Macavity number divinely, and of course the legendary Wayne Sleep was boggling our eyes and minds. Stephen Tate's transition from Gus, the Theatre Cat, to Growltiger was touching and impressive. Kenn Wells, a consummate artist, portrayed Skimbleshanks with great charm and verve. Bonnie Langford was a delight as Rumpleteazer, and her companion John Thornton overcame his injuries and assumed the role of Mungojerrie, as well as that of Macavity. There was the emergence of Susan Jane Tanner as a force to be reckoned with, not to mention the formidable presence of Roland Alexander as the dark dramatic Rumpus Cat, the angelic voice of John Chester and the pure magic of Finola Hughes. When I sang "The Moments of Happiness" for the first time, I was transfixed by the angelic voice that followed immediately after and gave the haunting melody of "Memory" its first airing in the show. The voice belonged to a young lady named Sarah Brightman.

In short the whole cast oozed talent but, as yet, certain parts of the show were not gelling and energies frequently misfired and fizzled out. Harry Rabinowitz was brought in to shake us into a greater awareness of the words and music. A celebrated conductor, full of wisdom and charm, he was nevertheless capable of jumping on your toes if you failed to pay attention.

Trevor Nunn also gave what were known as "solos" (head to heads). I loved them. On one such occasion he laughed long and quietly, as I expounded on Old Deuteronomy.

"I don't see him as Andrew does, as an old shrunken cat with spectacles, but rather as a big, gentle, wise Moses with a Buddhist quality — a big white lion!"

Trevor laughed even more, nodding all the while and repeating, "A big white lion."

The following morning, I was in early, before the rest of the cast, and was fortunate enough to watch Gilly Lynne dance the whole of the "Jellicle Ball". The "Jellicle Ball" closes the first half of the show and requires the dancers to dance non-stop for seventeen minutes. When she had finished, Lindsey on the piano roared "Bravo!", I too attempted to express my appreciation for her astonishing performance, but the words stuck in my mouth and I became consumed with shyness. I was also non-plussed as to why she had done it.

When at last we transferred to the New London Theatre, certain members of the cast complained that the "Jellicle Ball" was really far too strenuous. Gilly then repeated what I had witnessed in the rehearsal room. The demonstration left the cast speechless and Gilly cut through the silence saying, "Do you wish me to do it again?" Plaintive cries of "No, No" echoed round the theatre.

John Napier's set took our breath away. Never had a pile of rubbish been assembled so imaginatively! The momentum was now growing, as the "rubbish tip" was made a magic place by David Hersey's lighting. Jeff Shankley had returned; his knee was somewhat stiff, but it in no way detracted from his powerful portrayal of the Warrior Munkustrap. We were all keeping our fingers crossed for Judi's return.

We now did our first run-through, which was a complete disaster. Important onlookers, who had popped in to watch, must have been shocked at what they saw. We were not familiar with the complexities of the set, and the artists found themselves running out of space.

Periodically someone would fall off the stage. During one number, "The Pekes and the Pollicles", the dancers had a particularly bad time. They collided left, right and centre, because their headgear was as yet unfinished and they couldn't see where they were going! Sitting upstage centre, I ached with laughter. The odd bod would come up to me and enquire, "Where the bloody hell am I?"

After that dreadful rehearsal, Trevor and Gilly patiently set about solving the problems and we returned to an even keel. The orchestra was introduced, which was most exciting. In my case, it was also a little unnerving until I got used to it. This was my first experience singing with a full accompaniment and it was vastly different from singing simply with the piano!

Generally speaking, people were having good days and bad. Tension and fear mounted and then melted away again. The pressure of putting on a musical like this was enormous. The smallest problem escalates and upsets the whole. Gilly, for instance, still had a great deal of work to complete with the dancers. Every second of her time was taken up and we were worried that she was not getting enough sleep. Her fit, slim frame became even slimmer and her features looked strained. Her guts and will power, however, carried her through as, at last, she could see the light at the end of the tunnel.

John Napier, a very loveable man, on occasions exploded like a volcano at Trevor, as he poured out his misgivings. The tirade finished, I whispered in Trevor's ear, "Never mind. Ipswich Town are doing fine."

"Not true," he replied anxiously "One more bad result and they will be in danger of relegation."

I, in fact, was only trying to cheer him up. I had lost all track of the current season, my life having been totally swamped by this production. Trevor's work load, on the other hand, was the same, year in and year out, and he had obviously found ways and means of squeezing the football season into his busy schedule.

Andrew Lloyd Webber, driving himself as hard as anybody, was incensed one day when his secretary, Biddy, had been asked by a pianist to try to find a certain type of foot pedal for his piano. When she had acquired it, the pianist, on reflection, felt that after all he didn't really need it. On receiving this news, Andrew exploded onto the stage and into the orchestra pit, lit the blue touch paper, as befits a Chinese firecracker, and roared magnificently, "Now that Biddy has searched high and low for two days for the damn pedal, you can jolly well use the bloody thing! And another thing, I don't like the way you are playing my music, I don't recognise it. As for the strings, jolly well play up! You call that playing? Why do you let yourselves be drowned out by the brass? I've had just about as much as I can take today! Brian!" (Brian Brolly was his manager.) "Come with me." Andrew's long arm and finger pointed the way to the exit, and he swept out majestically.

Andrew is a perfectionist. He works and pushes himself unmercifully and, I think, demands these same standards of those who work with him. He passionately believes in and loves the British theatre.

Several days after this incident, one artist, who shall remain nameless, completely lost his rag and had a real go at Trevor Nunn. It was simply awful and I stood in the auditorium, horrified.

"You think I'm an idiot don't you? You know sweet fanny adams about music — don't give me all that crap. You think I'm thick. You think I'm not as intelligent as all those Shakespearian actors you usually work with. You don't listen to an effing thing I say. When it comes to musicals, you're a bloody non-starter. You patronise me every time you open your mouth. Well, I know what I'm talking about and I know how to put this number across!"

Throughout this tirade Trevor retained his composure, gently attempting to placate this very irate artist, who had misunderstood Trevor's ideas and objectives. The diatribe lasted for about fifteen minutes and destroyed any semblance of rehearsal for the rest of the morning.

Half-way up the auditorium, Trevor sat down, looking a bit drained. I planted a friendly arm on his shoulder and pushed a black coffee into his hand. He nodded a thank you and said softly, "God, Brian. This profession. There are times . . .," and his voice trailed away.

It was in moments like this that the stature of the man was evident. Trevor is the only man I have met (outside a certain sage) who is capable of such admirable control. He refused to identify with all these black moods and powered on. He clearly believes that negativity helps no one and is a waste of precious time. Time was short, it always is with musicals, and some scenes were still unrehearsed.

As well as Old Deuteronomy, I was playing Bustopher Jones, the "fat gigantic cat about town", a fine respected personage, resplendent with monocle, cigar and white spats, who, on the way to his favourite clubs and restaurants, condescends to look in on the riff-raff at the Jellicle Ball. This, too, was desperately under-rehearsed. My problem was that my main character, Old Deuteronomy, made his entrance shortly after Bustopher's exit and I was afraid that the two voices would sound similar. So, somewhere at the back of my mind, I had the germ of an idea. I wanted to give him a tiny voice, reminiscent of Burlington Bertie. But this never came to fruition. In the rush of those final days, it was never resolved. Trevor had worked out some highly imaginative business and Gilly taught me a funny walk to show off my white spats but I never managed to pull it off to my satisfaction. Indeed, there was barely time for me to work out my moves as Deuteronomy, and I constantly got in everybody's way, despite my eagerness to adapt to their dancing. Half blinded by the lights, as I meandered about the stage, I created havoc with every step. Gilly, choking back her laughter, would shout, "No, Golly, not there! You're blocking the view. No, no, no, keep to the side. Now, Golly, now — move in now! Sway to the music, take your time. Go back, go back. Sit down. Good. Stay there!"

The spirits of the team rose again, as we sped on towards opening night. It must be said that I was thoroughly enjoying myself and was given much help and encouragement by the other players. Wayne Sleep, on one occasion, sweetly instructed me in my clumsy attempts to pirouette gracefully! T. S. Eliot's wife, Valerie, was in attendance and generously offered assistance whenever we needed it. Harry Rabinowitz advised me that I was making the last song too heavy.

"But I'm singing the notes correctly," I countered.

"Yes, of course you are, but you are making them too brown. Lighten it."

With days ticking by and the theatre in a constant flurry of activity, the time loomed near for the first preview. Sitting on my customary giant car tyre at the back of the stage, I viewed the heaving mass of bodies in front of me as they performed one of the numbers. At one moment, as they separated and moved back, I looked through the dim light and saw the sweet frame of the mighty atom herself: Judi Dench. She had returned, sitting unobtrusively and looking endearingly vulnerable. We descended on her, almost killing her with hugs and kisses. Gillian, Andrew, Cameron and Trevor watched all this with smiles of relief. At the same time there was still concern for her weakened leg, as she had only just left the hospital. True to her spirit, great trooper that she is, Judi insisted that she would participate in the opening dance number, when the assembly of cats introduce themselves to the audience. Having remembered the moves, she had no difficulty in moulding in with the rest. The morning moved on and everyone sighed with relief.

At a certain moment, for some unaccountable reason, the rehearsal lights went off, plunging the stage into temporary darkness. At that moment Judi was walking across a small bridge, that spanned several seats at the front. The sickening thud, as she fell, reverberated around the auditorium. When the lights came back on, we viewed with consternation and horror her forlorn figure. Holding her head and leg, she wept with pain and unhappiness. Her despair at this final cruel blow was shared by us all, as we tried to comfort her. Trevor's arms were about her and, with our help, he carried her to her dressing room. The last image was of her distraught, tear-stained face, being held tenderly by Trevor, as the door slowly closed, bringing to an end her participation in the musical.

The next day, Trevor and Gilly clapped hands in unison, to galvanise the show back into action. They indicated the diminutive form alongside them and introduced us to that celebrated artist, Elaine Page. Elaine's broad smile prompted a warm response and we were on our way again!

The splendid Myra Sands would play the Gumbie Cat and Elaine would play Grizabella. She proved herself an accomplished dancer, learning the opening number in no time. Within two days her interpretation of the song "Memory" was tugging at the heart strings, as her great voice soared through the theatre.

The countdown had started and we were into the dress rehearsal. As is commonly accepted, dress rehearsals are almost always a shambles. Ours was something else! Timings were out; body mikes filled with sweat and wouldn't work. As I walked amongst the dancers during my numbers, they entreated me, "Please, Brian, press the bloody mike in, it's come out of its socket!"

"Sing, sing, sing," shouted Gilly, as Sharon Lee-Hill, having completed the marathon of the Jellicle Ball, had to plunge into a solo song. Sharon's body pulsated and throbbed, as she desperately tried to catch her breath and produce a sound.

"I — I — I can't. I — I can't," she puffed.

"It's all right," interrupted Trevor. "I'll rest you elsewhere."

Each and every dancer complained about the slipperiness of the stage, but Wayne Sleep, during his big solo dance as Magical Mr Mistoffolees outdid them all. The dance shoes he was wearing provided no grip at all and he staggered around the stage constantly hitting the floor. He stopped, stood still and, with the spotlight focused on him, held an imaginary conversation with someone in the auditorium. The show came to a complete stop.

"What, darling? Oh yes, darling, the shoes are absolutely gorgeous. Couldn't be better. I love ice skating. Oh yes, yes, yes, just look at me — up, down, up, down, hoppity there, hoppity here — one, two, three, fall — one, two, three, crash — Ring a Ring of Roses, Pocket Full of Poses. I'm absolutely delirious with happiness!"

At this point, he balanced on each leg in turn, tore off the shoes with frenzied emotion and threw them way out into the auditorium. "Take the bloody awful, shitty things and give them to some Russian farmer, who drives a bloody combined harvester!"

Throughout all this, the orchestra had stopped, but a lone drummer continued to tap, totally bewildered by it all! I was able to view the whole scenario objectively, from my car tyre at the centre of the stage. Despite the problems, there was no doubt in my mind that the talent and energy in the show was unique and that, as Cameron had said, all would be well.

When the final dress rehearsal had melted away, it meant that the first preview was at hand. With half an hour to go, the atmosphere backstage was like Vesuvius about to erupt. All the good souls jumped and jigged around incessantly and it became increasingly hard to bring order.

For the only time in my experience, Trevor swore. "Bloody hell, be quiet!" This change in tone had the desired effect and all was quiet and still.

"If you will only listen to me for five minutes, we will make this show a success. Please, please, keep still and give me your undivided attention."

As Trevor spoke, Wayne Sleep quietly commenced to tap dance around him.

"What are you doing?" Trevor enquired, staring incredulously.

"I'm not sure of the steps," Wayne replied.

The pause was long but our director stoically continued. "Brian sings the last song wonderfully, but you are not synchronising your movements with his words."

I'm afraid, at this point, I was so embarrassed at Trevor's praise, that I pretended a dead faint and collapsed on the floor. The cast jumped on me and simulated the act of copulation. It developed into a mountainous mass of seething bodies. Trevor's mood changed. He could see he was not going to win, so he searched the heap for my embarrassed face.

"You really are cracked, Brian," he said.

"Well, Trevor, even cats can be woofters!" spake I.

The evening was glorious. The combination of music, sound, lighting, orchestra, choreography, dancing, acting, sets and direction gelled into one great magnificent show. The titanic effort that Webber and MacKintosh had made to raise the money to put the show on, had paid off. As I finished the last song and looked down from the Heaviside Layer, higher even than the Russell Hotel, my eyes observed the panorama below me. Dancers bent double with exhaustion and commitment, screamed joyously, as only the young can. "We've done it! We've done it!" I was most moved.

The audience was almost out of control, stamping the floor and pounding their seats and erupting into uncontrolled roars of approval. As my rubber tyre descended, my eyes caught the solo figure of Andrew Lloyd Webber half hidden in the shadows near the vocal booth. His hands shivered convulsively, as he tried desperately to cope with his emotions. He was crying — uncontrollably.

It was virtually impossible to get the audience to go home. It seemed that the "Bravos" would go on forever. Gilly Lynne was incoherent, as she struggled in the arms of the loving cast. Only Cameron MacKintosh could find words. He smiled broadly and pumped everyone's hand vigorously. He was plainly thrilled.

"I told you it would work," he said.

In the stillness of the dressing room, removing my make-up, the tannoy system burst into life and the voice of Trevor Nunn came through: "Dear Company, with all my heart I thank you for what you have achieved tonight. Your performance was truly great and fills me with pride. Thank you, thank you very much."

Of course, the rest is history. The first night of *Cats* proved to be a phenomenal success and now productions of it have been mounted throughout the world. As I write, an Eskimo on the holiday programme is playing "Memory" on a banjo in the farthest reaches of Alaska. But it was that first preview that has etched itself deep in my "memory".

Time shot by and I was astonished to realise that I had been in the show for over two years. On finally descending for the last time, in my tyre, from the Heaviside Layer, I saw a slim figure in a blue shirt on my left. Of course, it was Trevor. Standing by my side and holding my hand tightly, he gave a moving graceful speech to the audience, expressing his appreciation for my efforts. He turned and looked at me. Then the Ipswich Town Football Club supporter smiled and led off the celebrations.

CHAPTER
EIGHT

Mr & Mrs Davidson

I suppose the most challenging, the most surprising, the most daring and the most everything else adventure we ever take in all our lives is to marry And how little we realise this at the time.

As time goes by, we wonder, in retrospect, how we ever had the courage to do it. Did we know how much energy and dedication marriage needs to simply survive, let alone what patience, kindness and delicacy we need to achieve balance, harmony, security, peace and happiness?

Weddings are the most exciting, joyful and hopeful of all occasions, especially if the bride and groom are particularly dear to you, and so in December 1987 I was very, very happy to be travelling to Scotland to attend the wedding of John-Paul Davidson to his chosen bride-to-be, Margaret Magnusson. J.P. is quite simply the man who made my dreams come true. He is also the leading man in this chapter.

Just twelve months earlier I was in a frightful state, very low and frustrated — a new experience for me, for I pride myself on being a born optimist. You see I simply could not raise the money for the Everest project, the film that we finally did make in 1990, called "Galahad of Everest".

Throughout the Seventies I had plagued film producers, directors and anyone who would listen to me. I was patronised, fobbed off, turned down flat, encouraged by leads that went nowhere. There were now no more irons in the fire. Nothing whichever way I looked. My dream had ground to a halt.

George Leigh Mallory, the subject of my proposed film, was nicknamed "Sir Galahad" and on the night of 23 December 1986 I stood outside London's Kensington Hilton Hotel, musing how deeply the project needed such "a knight". I was waiting to meet a BBC producer/director. As I looked up the lights of the steady stream of cars dimmed a little and there, on the brow of the hill appeared the single clear light of a lone steed. I focused intently on it as it drew nearer and entered the forecourt of the hotel. The rider reined in, in full control of the magnificent beast, which snorted uneven breaths before at last its eye faded and died. The tall slim figure in black dismounted from his charger and removed his black helmet, his dark eyes viewing me all the while with quiet amusement.

"Hello, I'm John-Paul Davidson," a clear young voice announced.

I did not know it at the time but here indeed was the very Galahad I had been looking for. We shook hands warmly and made swiftly for the eating place suggested by my new champion. Once there, by the soft clear light of the table lamp, I was able to observe him in greater detail.

He was about six feet tall, though his slimness made him appear taller. His face was a delicate pale, full and yet devoid of excess weight, and his sharp cheek bones highlighted his ultra-sensitive expression. The eyes, high-set eyebrows and slightly thinning hair, all seemed black. His deep-set eyes were the clue to his nature, alternating between a mature intensity and the look of a child of five.

The evening went splendidly and John-Paul, or J.P. as he preferred to be called, felt that there was just a faint possibility that the Everest project could be pulled off! Later we headed back to the Kensington Hilton. There "Sir Galahad" placed his black helmet firmly on his head, mounted his steed, and extended his hand to me in knightly friendship. Then he gracefully spurred his charger into motion, reined in slightly, threw me a handsome salute and sped off into the night.

Over the coming months and years, J.P.'s companion-ship, enterprise, intelligence and unflagging faith and support sustained me, as, together now, we pursued producers, bankers and television companies. I never again despaired because, now, at last, I had a "believer".

It transpired later that he was to marry a lady by the name of Margaret Magnusson, our chapter's leading lady. When J.P. introduced me to his bride-to-be, I was delighted, as J.P.'s happiness was of great importance to me and (should I have doubted?) he had chosen so well. Margaret was as pretty as a picture, with striking natural blonde hair, a fair complexion, dazzling blue eyes and a perfect slim figure to match. She was a bundle of energy. Possessed of a no-nonsense open nature, she didn't suffer fools gladly. The essence of her personality was honesty. Within seconds of entering a room, she showed all the clarity and coolness of her Icelandic forefathers, combined with the special warmth and colour of Scotland. She was a force to be reckoned with.

Gradually, the wedding day drew near and the prospect delighted me. It was to take place in Scotland and I had never been to Scotland!

"What shall I wear?" I asked Margaret dubiously.

"What will you wear, indeed!" She retorted. "What you always wear! Yer great baggy sweater! Please, Brian. Don't fuss yerself, wear what you like. . . . At least it'll get your mind, and John-Paul's for that matter, off Everest. How on earth your wife tolerates your obsession I do not know! John-Paul is bad enough. I think the pair of you are small boys who will never grow up!"

She was absolutely right, we were little boys and there was little prospect of us ever growing up.

And so, shortly after Christmas 1987 I drove up the colourless motorway and headed for "Bonnie Scotland". How odd, I mused, that J.P. was to marry on the 28th of December. Hildegard and I had married on the 28th of December nine years earlier, just a simple registry office affair but I was very nervous and cocked up what I was supposed to say completely. It's a pretty long legal rigmarole in registry offices and I think I changed the word "lawful" to "unlawful" amongst other mistakes. There had been a bit of a pause, while the registrar wondered whether he should make me say it all again.

He must have decided it was unwise, as we might be there all day trying to get it right! I think he was mesmerised to find this well-known actor quite unable to say his lines. Hildegard always says that we were not really properly married as a result.

I broke my journey in South Yorkshire near Doncaster, to see my mum and dad in Bolton-On-Dearne. Both were in excellent spirits, as always. Although my mother had been ill for many years, she soldiered on gamely, never complaining. My father, except for the odd chest pain, was as hale and hearty as ever. They were both now in their eighties and I loved them more than ever.

As I looked at their dear faces at the dinner table, I contemplated their marriage, now some sixty years in duration. My mother's childhood was unspeakably deprived, even by the standards reigning early this century in a Yorkshire mining town. I will not go into detail, as it is her story and I have no right to intrude. But it must have been a Blessed day indeed, when Dad appeared, not on a white charger, it was black I'm sure, black as the coal he hewed daily down the pit. A Blessed day for him too. As I looked at her dear face, I remembered eating well throughout the war and after during the rationing only because Mother ate so little. My father, Alan and I were always so lovingly cared for.

What a fine marriage. What a success, when you consider how great a struggle it must have been. A struggle that my brother Alan and I were protected from, leaving us free to run and breathe and grow up.

When I visit my family, I always stay with Mum and Dad, in what used to be my room in my childhood. Mum always retires early, while Dad and I talk until the small hours. The following morning, it's always around the corner to Alan and Ann, my sister-in-law. What do I say about her? She is the soul of love, kindness and gentleness and they have been sweethearts, since their teens.

For many years now, Alan has suffered from an assortment of ailments, from bronchial trouble to severe back problems. He is all but an invalid and retired prematurely from being a school supervisor. But he has a load of guts and a love of life. Never have I met anyone so cheerful. I just miss those days when I could grab hold of him and wrestle him to the ground. It is ridiculous that I should be so healthy and he so ill. Still, in spite of all this, he is happy.

Life is so strange. Having to retire so young would seem a tragic event but Alan and Ann have turned this around into a positive and happy period of their lives. They are a potent duo. Because of his disabilities, he is the brains and she is the brawn, the only woman I know who can "brickie" with the best of 'em. After a week's "holiday" here with Hildegard and me, our home is transformed, the shed neat and tidy, the fish pond clear and the lawn as smooth and beautiful as any golf course green. Their family is so close-knit you cannot see the stitches. Generally when they leave us it is because *we* have to do a Geography project, which Ilona, their daughter, has to hand in at the beginning of term or *we* have to practise the piano, as Neil, their son, has a concert on such and such a day.

And so, after breakfast, reflecting on these two marriages, and after many hugs and kisses, I motored off to Scotland and J.P. and Margaret's big day. It is said that Scotland is God's country but on this occasion, it was showing its wet side. Rain hit my car from all sides, as I approached the outskirts of Glasgow.

The couple were to be married some thirty miles further on in a remote castle-like church, as befits such a knight as Sir Galahad and his lady. Glasgow's architecture looked beautiful and pristine, the result of a fine restoration programme. The people were kind and helpful, taking all the time in the world to explain to me how to get to my destination. Then, after driving for a while on gorgeous winding roads past numerous waterfalls and flashing streams, I was there.

The wedding was like no other I'd ever been to. The building I surmised was fourteenth century, certainly it was very old. The large central hall was impressive, yet warm and inviting and filled with flowers of every description.

Wet through and looking singularly unimpressive, I was ushered to my seat near the front by a young man, immaculately dressed in a green tartan kilt.

"Glad you could come," he whispered. "They will be pleased. Good heavens, Mr Blessed! Steam is coming off you, I hope you don't catch cold!"

Glancing around the gathering, my eyes focused on Magnus Magnusson, Margaret's father and her family and J.P.'s mother and friends, all beaming with expectation. The vicar, stocky of frame, white-haired,

red-faced and possessed of a fine, sensitive, strong voice, began the sacred ceremony. I became aware of numerous children in the throng. Unabashed by the solemnity of the occasion they whooped and shouted happily. You could see the delight in the vicar's eyes, for him and everyone present, this was what weddings were all about. Behind me, the pipes played their joyful ancient rhythm, heralding the entrance of the groom himself, J.P.

Resplendent in tartan kilt, as was the best man, he walked and swayed to the call of the pipes. His face was pale and serious but broke fleetingly into a nervous smile. Shyly he turned his eyes, in unison with everyone else, to a vision of never to-be-forgotten loveliness, as Margaret appeared mystically through the far portal of the hall.

She moved effortlessly and the subtle combination of her white gown, fair complexion and natural blonde hair brought a gasp of admiration from the congregation. The magic was enhanced by the outriders, her bridesmaid and a little page-boy in tartan trews and a tam o'shanter.

On reaching the altar, Margaret smiled confidently and gloriously at J.P., who bit his lip and stared. The vicar's voice guided them and us gravely and simply through the always beautiful ceremony. His voice echoed around the church and entwined all our hearts and minds in joy and celebration of the love of John-Paul for Margaret and Margaret for John-Paul. A cherub, in the guise of a baby boy, broke ranks, left his distracted parents and on all fours, motored round the couple as they made their vows, intent on some object beyond the altar. I caught the ghost of a smile

from Magnus Magnusson, as he relished the moment.
Of course, J.P. and Margaret were quite unaware of
the small interloper, their joined hands trembling with
emotion and concentration. To the gorgeous amusement
of the onlookers, J.P. asked the Vicar: "Could you repeat
that please? I didn't quite hear it . . ."

Then the lovely ceremony reached its climax. There
was laughter and tears from the happy parents and
relatives, as the bride and groom kissed poignantly.
Then it was time for the cameras. All was frantic
mayhem, as everyone vied for a position from which
to photograph the couple. The wild wind outside played
havoc with hats, veils and dresses, as the throng milled
about and called out instructions.

"Over here, please, Margaret. . . ."

"Look here, J.P. . . ."

"May we have the bride on her own please? . . . Ah,
that's lovely!"

"You look lovely!"

"Could we have the attendants as well now please?"

"I'd like the groom and the best man!"

Finding myself hemmed in, I jockeyed for a position
on a high wall and, balancing somewhat precariously, I
proceeded to film with my "Video 8" camera. Despite
the velocity of the wind and the close attention of the
crowd, Margaret remained the picture of composure.

During a lull in the proceedings, she sped through the
admirers to the graveyard opposite, to pay her respects
to a departed dear one. Maggie had lost her brother
Siggy, when he was only eleven years old. He was
killed in a road accident. The onlookers kept their

distance, respecting her privacy. Had it not been for the slight movement of her dress and the trailing white arm enfolded by J.P, you would have sworn she was a marble statue. The image of her romantic, ghost-like figure, contrasting starkly with the dark gravestones and grey sky, will always stay with me. Edging closer and unnoticed by anyone, I ran the risk of being irreverent and filmed it all.

After a few moments, Margaret smiled and skipping lightly alongside the running groom, she re-joined the throbbing throng and posed again for the remaining frustrated photographers. Then it was cars, cars, cars from all directions, doors opening and banging shut, as the happy pilgrims set off to the eagerly awaited dinner, dance and entertainment some five miles or so distant. Running and scrambling over walls like a confused gorilla, I tried to get ahead of the revellers to achieve a continuous storyline for my film. All in vain, I'm afraid, as limousines of the most impressive kind outclassed me in skill and speed, leaving "Yours Truly" and my gentle automobile wet and steamed up.

Arriving at last at the large, warm, colourful hall that splendidly housed the revellers, I chatted happily with all the hard-working staff, whose unstinting efforts to make the occasion successful had gained my attention.

"The weather has nay helped," said a sweet, plump young lady, in black uniform dress and appropriate white pinafore, "but nair mind, all's well that ends well!"

Her cheerfulness was echoed by several "Ayes" from her companions, as they applied the finishing touches to food, napkins and flowers. Their enthusiasm and dexterity resulted in an excellent, beautifully coordinated banquet, that was much appreciated by all. There was food and drink in abundance.

People enjoyed themselves unreservedly. There was much laughter and their voices rang out, loud and free. Faces red and merry toasted the happy couple again and again. Speeches ranged from the short to the very long, and our hands were red-raw from clapping so much. It was such a joy for us all to celebrate a "match made in heaven". I noticed the little cherub, who had gone round the altar on all fours earlier, having a rare old time with the chocolate dessert. Half of it had found his gurgling mouth, the rest was spread across his face. During rests for belches, he catapulted spoonfuls onto the dresses and faces of his contemporaries. Avoiding the missiles were those two stalwarts of the BBC, Alan Yentob, Head of BBC2, and Jonathan Powell, the Head of BBC1.

During a speech of fine wit and fun, Yentob praised J.P.'s record as a producer of documentaries, mentioning that he first started with the BBC on the "Holiday Programme". "In fact," Yentob said, "J.P.'s enthusiasm for the 'Holiday Programme' knew no bounds, particularly the South of France, which was much appreciated by the aforementioned gentleman. Over a period of time, it was noticeable that, though the programme embraced the world, the central Loire Valley, Provence and the far reaches of Southern France were exceptionally well featured." He went on to joke that he had high hopes of persuading J.P. to commit his energies once again to programmes on that much neglected region.

J.P. rose amid laughter, thanked Yentob for his deliberations and said he would certainly give his suggestion some serious consideration. Then he described how difficult it had been to gain the hand of his bride; she was a lady who was more than a match for "Sir Galahad". The wooing of her required the crossing of many moats and drawbridges and the scaling of battlements, not to mention tasks of truth and commitment. After solving the riddles of mind and etiquette, he was, at last, accepted and never was there a happier man.

Several hours later, I reluctantly left that jovial celebration, as work beckoned in London. The cabaret entertainment had just begun, provided by the guests themselves. Outside, in the dark night, I peered through the windows, like Heathcliff looking at Cathy at Thrush Cross Grange in *Wuthering Heights*. The girls in their pretty dresses and the handsome young men eyed each other amid much gaiety. There was charm and warmth in the lights and the homespun musicians strummed a merry tune. J.P. and Margaret, radiating happiness, led the way with a Scottish jig and each step brought joy to every face in the hall.

"Hand in hand here we go, heel for heel and toe for toe . . ."

J.P. and Margaret are now striding confidently together through that other huge minefield — parenthood. They have two glorious boys — Robbie and Callum.

CHAPTER
NINE

The House of God

After *Cats*, I poured my energy into attempting to mount the film about George Leigh Mallory, his splendid companions and their historic endeavours to climb Mount Everest in the early 1920s. During this period the famous climber, Christian Bonington, asked, "What is the precise objective of the film, Brian?"

"Well, Chris, I can do no better than to quote what I have already written in the treatment: 'This expedition and film are devoted to conveying, as precisely as possible, the exact story as reported in the expedition books of the 1920s. We are not attempting to solve the mystery of Mallory and Irvine's last climb. Indeed, we feel mystery is a rare commodity today and we are most certainly not grave-digging. We simply wish to pay tribute to a great man and his magnificent companions. What better way than to follow in their footsteps.'"

The general consensus was that the whole enterprise was impossible and that I was bonkers. This negative attitude brought out my old stubbornness.

"Nothing's impossible!" was my passionate response.

I used the word "we" in the treatment because I now had a true friend, who backed me up loyally — J.P.

Nevertheless, any chance of mounting the film was as remote as ever. Day in, day out, I experienced hope followed by despair, as I was promised much but received nothing. Raising money for our film was the most distressing experience of my life. In the end Hildegard could take it no longer. Cornering me in the kitchen one day, she exclaimed, "Brian! I can't listen to you any longer, I think you should go and do something! It's time you stopped talking and climbed something. You don't even know whether you can do it anymore. Take Geoff Arkless and go to Kilimanjaro. It will do you (and me!) the world of good!"

This unexpected assault spurred me into action. Before too long, together with Cathy, my daughter from my first marriage, and my longtime friend and climbing mentor, Geoff, I found myself on a flight to the Dark Continent and Kilimanjaro.

In spite of an outward show of calm, Geoff's eyes revealed an inner excitement and I shared his feelings at the prospect of Kilimanjaro, the highest mountain in Africa (19,340 feet). But if we were excited, then Cathy, seated beside me on the plane, was more so. Her large, dark brown eyes flashed handsomely, as she savoured every moment.

Our plan was a simple one: on arrival at Kilimanjaro airport, we would proceed some twenty-five miles to the village of Marangu, situated at the base of Mount Kilimanjaro. Arrangements had been made through a travel company to stay at the Marangu Hotel, owned by the legendary Miss Erica Von Lany, one of the first women to climb the mountain when she was only thirteen years old! The equally impressive Mrs Brice-Bennett helped her to run the hotel.

A delightful surprise was that J.P. and Margaret, who were on honeymoon in Kenya, were to join us at Marangu and attempt to climb the mountain with us. Afterwards, they would continue on safari, Cathy would go to Mombasa and Geoff and I would proceed to Nairobi to climb Mount Kenya. In fact, I mooted to Geoff that I hoped the pair of us might be able to cross the border into Uganda and have a go at Ruwenzori, situated in the Mountains of the Moon. All this was possible, as we were staying for six and a half weeks.

If we couldn't get to Uganda, I was all for attempting one of the harder routes on Kilimanjaro, possibly the Heim or Kirstein Glacier, descending down the Great Western Breach Wall. Maybe we could have a look at the climb that the great Reinhold Messner did on the Breach Wall. Maybe we could . . .?

At this point Geoff diplomatically interrupted me. "Mr Blessed, Sir, I think you're possibly jumping the gun. All manner of things will dictate how we get on. Weather conditions on the mountain, the strength of the party, crossing borders, even filling in forms — anything could detain us. We'll just have to wait and see."

"Wait and see!" I muttered. "You look and sound like an ancient great aunt, crossed with a dried old prune!"

The corners of Geoff's mouth twitched, suggesting a smile, as he replied, "Ah well, we can't all be good looking, talented and as famous as yerself, Mr Blessed. What's it like, from your great height, looking down on us mortals?"

"In your case, thoroughly puzzling," I replied. "I sometimes wonder if you really exist! Guessing your weight is difficult. I would say you're somewhere between five pounds and eight stone."

No response.

"How old are you?" I continued.

"I stopped counting years ago."

"Do you have a sex life?" I droned on.

"Daddy!" Cathy interjected. "The whole aeroplane can hear you!"

"It's all right, we're quite enjoying it," was the response from various seats.

Excitement abounded on the aircraft, as almost everyone was embarking on some kind of safari or adventure. Hildegard was right, it was doing me the world of good.

Seven hours later, we were there. Standing on the aircraft steps, we were enveloped by tremendous heat and the seductive perfume of nearby flowers and shrubs. Then, far away, almost on the horizon, I saw Mount Kilimanjaro. The Masai tribesmen call it "The House of God" and, indeed, the ancient volcano seemed to float, suspended in the sky, cut off from the earth by a fleecy belt of cloud at its base. Even at this range I could distinguish the Kirstein and Heim glaciers.

Once through the complexities of customs, we took our time, feasting our eyes on the spectacle. Periodically, the clouds dispersed, revealing another of the Great One's secrets. There, shimmering and vibrating surrealistically above the Shira Plateau, was the Arrow

Glacier, highlighted by the darkness of the rock. Oh, to be there!

"God, Geoff!" I exclaimed. "It's absolutely sensational!"

In the stillness of the afternoon we stood there, rooted to the spot, transfixed by the vision. However, we were quickly brought back to earth by the hard bargaining of the taxi driver.

"Forty dollars, Sir?"

"No!" Geoff replied. "Twenty."

The customary compromise was reached — thirty dollars it was!

The ride from the airport was dusty but exciting. The red soil of the countryside contrasted vividly with the green of the vegetation and, as we travelled through the busy town of Arusha and on to Marangu, the mountain hovered tantalisingly closer. Then we were at the Marangu Hotel. What a heavenly place!

We cooed like doves as the old-world charm of the residence relaxed our minds. The central courtyard was surrounded by low-lying white buildings with faded red corrugated roofs and green painted windows. Manicured bushes contrasted charmingly with the large rubber plants and rampant creepers that ran riot over the houses. From these plants sprouted red hibiscus and a myriad of coloured flowers. Against a back-drop of brilliant red oleander, two large white turkeys squabbled for the attention of a local Wachagga who, with dark skin glistening and white teeth flashing, shook with glee at the antics of the birds.

Outside the courtyard were dozens of little white

houses scattered over fifty acres or more. Light brown cows grazed on the thick carpet of grass that surrounded the building. The grace and tranquility of the setting was enhanced by the multitude of birds: ducks, geese, hens, pigeons and species that I had never seen the like of in my life, all pottered around the ferns in a riot of ecstasy. My goodness, it felt like Day One on earth. Just as we felt our senses could take no more, through the high trees in the evening light, the snows of Kilimanjaro turned breathtakingly gold.

"Mr Blessed? Please forgive me for interrupting you. My name is Mrs Brice-Bennett."

It was a lady in her mid-fifties, handsome and refined of feature, upright and dignified of stature and warm and sophisticated in manner. With a spirited glint in her eye, her face broke into a wry smile, as she extended her hand in friendly greeting.

"Welcome to Marangu. I'm sorry that Miss Von Lany isn't here to say hello. No doubt you'll see her tomorrow. In the meantime, we will show you all to your quarters. I do hope that you'll be comfortable. In a short while, you will hear a gong heralding dinner. This way, please."

In due course, as the big tropical sun kissed the hillsides goodnight and disappeared, the soft sound of the gong serenaded us to dinner. The subtle lights of the dining room revealed the many pictures on the white walls, each one depicting different landscapes on the mountain.

The meal was simple and scrumptious. After vegetable soup, the main course consisted of tasty new potatoes, beef, sweet carrots, peas and oodles of fine, rich gravy. A great variety of fruit was then presented and coffee was taken at leisure in the adjoining large study room. All the while, we were cosseted with great charm by the charismatic Wachagga, who live on the slopes of the mountain.

Relishing the pure ground coffee, the three of us eased our bodies into the soft cushions of our large armchairs. Ah, what bliss! What comfort! In six days' time it would be entirely different but, for the moment, the three explorers were entitled to wallow in unashamed luxury.

Before turning in we marvelled at the tropical night sky. Never had I seen the galaxy so devastatingly impressive. Its millions of stars, blue, green, red and white, shone brilliantly.

"Ah, Cathy," I sighed longingly. "The whole of the Milky Way must be teeming with life."

"Oh yes," she responded with a smile. "And beyond!"

That night, three extremely contented heads hit their pillows, while the fireflies and their companions hummed them to sleep.

It was to be five days before J.P. and Margaret arrived, and the time was taken up with reading, gongs, breakfasts, lunches, dinners, walks and exercise. Marangu is at 4,000 feet, therefore a teeny-weeny bit of acclimatisation takes place.

Drawn by the thought of going higher, I would lazily meander up to the Marangu Gate at 6,000 feet; I was chomping at the bit to get on with the climb. One day, on the way down, I turned off the road and went through the trees towards the distant sound of water.

After a few hundred yards, I came to a small rocky valley, full of gentle, picturesque waterfalls. Naked Wachagga children, in deliriums of delight, swam and dived inexhaustibly in the deep pools.

A score of very tiny tots, their bodies covered in mud from the poolside, motored on all fours up the embankment. Giggling away, they failed to notice that they were heading straight towards me. When they came face to face with my pale features and large beard, they were thunderstruck. Never have I seen faces so open-mouthed, frozen and horrified. The nearest lad, who couldn't have been more than three, blurted out: "Simba!"

Immediately they all took up the cry. "Simba! Simba! Simba!"

This, of course, means Lion. They had obviously never seen a white man at such close quarters before, and certainly not one with such a beard. They were quite convinced that I was some kind of cross between a lion and a human. For the next hour they followed me in droves, keeping their distance and chanting rhythmically "Simba" and hooting with laughter when I obligingly roared at them. From then on I was greeted with the name wherever I went.

At last, J.P. and Margaret arrived from Kenya. Two days later, after a series of swims and walks, we found ourselves seated, in company with several strangers, in the coffee room, mesmerised by Miss Erica Von Lany. This lady was somewhat older than Mrs Brice-Bennett and she used a walking stick to aid her in her daily activities. Her grey hair was swept back neatly. Her delicate bell-like voice and sophisticated manner were intriguing. On an easel before us was a large painting of Kilimanjaro, showing the tourist route which we would be taking, and she used her walking stick to point the way.

"Firstly, you will gather at reception to meet your individual porters. You will be going to a great height and we strongly advise that you don't carry anything of weight — that is the job of your porter. He is used to it and he is acclimatised.

"Throughout the climb we recommend *pola-pola* — slowly, slowly. If you attempt to go fast, you run the risk of becoming seriously ill, with either pulmonary oedema or cerebral oedema. Please take this warning seriously. The graveyard in Marangu contains many people who have not heeded this.

"Climbing Kilimanjaro will prove most uncomfortable if you do not use a stick. These will be provided for you in due course. Now, your journey.

"You will be driven to Marangu Gate at 6,000 feet. From there your adventure begins. First you walk through fascinating tropical rain forest. The sights and sounds that greet you here are truly amazing. They include exotic flowers of every description — multi-coloured bird life, butterflies, monkeys and many, many other creatures. Your porters will go ahead of you to prepare your meals, so please stay strictly to the well-worn path, as there is always the possibility that you could encounter such creatures as the African wild dog.

"After three or four hours, you will arrive at the

Mandara Huts at 9,000 feet, at the top of the rain forest. They consist of a central wooden chalet surrounded by smaller huts, with accommodation for about two hundred people. Here, you will spend the night.

"From Mandara, the following day, you will follow a steep path through the mighty heath forest. Then the scenery changes dramatically and you will behold the giant lobelia. Emerging from this and veering left, you travel northwest across the moorlands of the southern slopes of Mawenzi, the easterly subsidiary summit, finally arriving at the Horombo Huts, at 12,000 feet: distance, fourteen kilometres — time, five hours.

"Ascending the next day, you will proceed up the valley behind the Horombo Huts and on to the saddle between Mawenzi and Kibo, the main summit. Here, you will begin to feel the altitude, as you are at 14,000 feet.

"Having passed the fascinating Zebra Rocks, you will reach a rain gorge. Once more, the landscape changes, this time into a desert region. The left-hand path at the rain gorge crosses the saddle on its western side and leads, on rocky terrain, to the Kibo Hut on the eastern slopes of Kibo itself. You are now at 15,200 feet, and you will feel it.

"In all probability, you will suffer from headaches and breathlessness. It is advisable to take a little aspirin to aid sleep. If you are unwell, have the good sense to turn back, for now the going is tough.

"It is normal to leave the Kibo Hut by 3 a.m. One of the blessed advantages of this is that it is so dark you don't see the endless scree slopes before you. Remember, *pola-pola* — please go slowly.

"You will now follow a well defined path behind the hut. As it is dark, your torches will be on and the guides will be leading the way. After about two hours, you will reach a large overhang, Hans Meyer Cave. The hardest part is here, as you zig-zag straight up steep scree to the crater rim at Johannes Notch and left to Gillman's Point, at over 18,000 feet. It is advisable here to take a rest, as you really have conquered the climb.

"You must all sign the Gillman's Point record book. Those of you who feel like it can then continue round the crater rim, through snow and arctic conditions on the ice cap to the summit, Uhuru, or Freedom Peak, at 19,340 feet. You will have had the unique experience of climbing through tropical, alpine and arctic zones.

"It is customary to come down quite quickly, not staying at the Kibo Hut, but continuing on to the Horombo Hut, where you will spend your last night on the mountain. The next day you will arrive at the Marangu Gate and then back here to the hotel."

At this point Miss Erica Von Lany paused, wiped her brow and added, "And you'll wonder why you ever did it!"

On leaving the meeting, I bumped into Mrs Brice-Bennett. "Have you climbed the mountain?" I asked.

"Yes," she replied. "Once. And that was enough!"

The next morning, at about 10 a.m., in company with our designated porters, we commenced the climb. Everyone was in good spirits. Margaret and Cathy smiled broadly and looked very fetching in their light alpine gear. Cathy was a little apprehensive, as she had never climbed a mountain before.

I regaled her with stories of Kilimanjaro mythology, to engage her imagination. Just around the corner from the hotel are several engraved rocks. Some believe they are examples of primitive art, whilst others link them to tribal ceremonies, such as initiating young males into the mysteries of manhood.

Any concern that Cathy had about altitude I smoothed with calming words. "Oh, there's no problem! We'll simply take it easy."

Therefore, it was a complete shock, at about 7,000 feet in the rain forest, to come across four Wachagga tribesmen carrying a stretcher with a large white man on it. And I mean large! He wasn't dissimilar in physique to Garth in the comic strip. Also, I must make a correction: the white man was now pale purple in colour.

"Jumbo Bwana," said one of the bearers, who bore a close resemblance to the black sergeant in the film *Where No Vultures Fly*.

I'm ashamed to say I had a fit of the giggles. The man's deep base voice reminded me of Paul Robeson. The whole scene was straight out of *Sanders of the River* or a Tarzan film. "Jumbo Simba," said another Wachagga, recognising me.

Then, to aggravate my fit of giggles, Geoff added his own high-pitched Geordie accent to the proceedings, with his "Jumbo".

When I finally managed to control myself, I asked what had happened.

"He's dying, Simba," replied the sergeant. "Cerebral

oedema." The sergeant then acted out cutting his throat and made gurgling noises, making it clear that death was imminent for the unfortunate fellow.

"Is there anything we can do?" I asked.

"No, Simba. This man, he is 'not get well'."

With that, they left. All of this had not escaped Cathy, who stared at me in horror.

"Ah, the man was obviously a piss-artist, unfit and had rushed up the mountain." I said to her. "There's no chance of us getting oedema!"

This experience certainly didn't fill us with confidence, but soon all negative thoughts were put behind, as the magic of the forest enchanted us once more.

There were eight in our party, the other three being New Zealanders — and great company they were too. The eldest, a tall slim man in his forties, was Bob Harvey, a TV executive. He had brought his 19-year-old gangling son, Frazer, with him. Completing this breezy threesome was their cheerful friend, Stewart, an athlete in his mid-twenties. I gathered Bob was very proud of the fact that he had equalled Lord Byron's feat of having swum the Hellespont. He had always yearned to climb Kilimanjaro.

Pola-pola — slowly — slowly we gained height. All that Miss Erica Von Lany had foretold was breathtakingly revealed. At last, there was the smoke of the Mandara Huts. Here we put on our red Comic Relief noses which J.P. filmed on "Video 8". This was to be sent to Lenny Henry at the BBC, for the African part of his charity show.

Day Two proved to be full of variety. One moment we

would peel off our garments, as the tropical sun blazed, and the next we would hurriedly replace them, as the rain and even sleet poured down upon us. The wind could be very fresh, coming, as it seemed, from the vicinity of the ice-cap. Then out would come the sun again, bathing us in its glory and inspiring us to have a picnic of boiled eggs, sandwiches, fruits and tea. What a great time!

We were now at an altitude of 10,000 feet. The astonishing giant lobelia and large ground heather dominated the scene everywhere. Alpine plants in Europe are noted for their delicacy and prettiness. Here the Alpine zone is gigantic, as if some great titan had done the gardening.

It is difficult to grasp the sheer size of this mountain; it's about two hundred miles wide, with its summit some 4,000 feet higher than anything in the Alps. As we approached the Horombo Huts at 12,000 feet, the terrain changed again, this time to its desert region. The eye could now travel a great distance. To our left, Tanzania's broad plain stretched out seemingly forever.

The sun's rays dazzlingly pierced the dark purple sky, creating golden laser beams of light which reached down to the earth below. The sun-scorched land, thus blindingly lit up, contrasted vividly with the dark clouds, as that other element, the azure sky, fleetingly revealed itself.

Cathy breathed, "I've never seen such a spectacle!"

It reminded me of the words of D. G. Rossetti: "Yet for this hour I still may be hereby stayed, and see the golden air and the silver fade, and the last bird fly into the last night . . ."

I have failed to mention, amidst this deluge of wonder, that Margaret had been the star of the ascent, exhibiting a style of climbing that, in originality, might prove interesting to Sir Edmund Hillary himself. Like her husband, she stubbornly insisted on carrying a rucksack, totally against the orders of Miss Von Lany. To alleviate the strain on her back and hips, she assumed the position of a chimpanzee, moving on all fours; the stooping position apparently gave her some relief. Nevertheless, she was happy and moved along like a two-year-old.

The push the next day for the Kibo Hut was a different story. As we made our way into the famous saddle between Mawenzi and Kibo, the altitude began to be felt in earnest. Everyone was noticeably struggling at 14,000 feet. Bob, though still smiling, frequently bent over in agony, whilst his son Frazer exclaimed, "Bloody hell, Dad. It's murder!"

The athlete, Stewart, dourly pressed on but complained of a headache, and Margaret was suffering from nausea. J.P., in spite of a headache, insisted he was fine, although his head tended to roll from side to side. Geoff seemed strong but had a bad cough. My delight in the adventure and obsession to go high seemed to override everything somehow and to protect me from the effects of the altitude. Geoff observed laconically, "Ah, I see Sir Brian is above such inconveniences!"

"You're just jealous, you old prune!" I replied.

My eyes were fixed on Cathy, who was making a valiant effort to keep going, as she so dearly wanted to get up. I kept shouting to J.P. to slow down; he is such a fast walker and I was worried that he was overdoing it. Margaret, too, was moving ahead of us and my shouts to her to slow down also went unheeded.

"I want to get to the Kibo Hut, so I can lie down," she shouted back.

At this point Cathy, walking alongside me, suddenly felt faint and, with Geoff assisting me, we sat her down. She whispered, "I don't feel sick, Daddy. It's just this strange pain at the side of my head and my hand hurts."

On examination, we discovered it was swollen.

"I think we should consider going down," said Geoff.

"No, no, no!" Cathy said. "Nothing of the kind! I'm not sick. Let me rest. I know it will pass. Please, I want to go on."

"We'll stay here as long as you like," I said. "Drink plenty of liquid, take a couple of aspirin and then see how you are feeling."

We were now at about 14,500 feet and we could see the well worn path leading to the Kibo Hut. There can be no doubt that ascending from 4,000 feet at Marangu, to the summit of Kilimanjaro at 19,340 feet in four days is terribly unwise. I strongly recommend to anyone attempting it that they stay two days at the Horombo Hut and the same period at Kibo. It will make the enterprise much safer and far more comfortable.

Much to my relief, after a considerable time, Cathy showed distinct signs of improvement. Taking great care, we edged our way up to the Kibo Hut. On arrival,

I gave her a great hug, pointing out that she had attained 15,200 feet, the highest of her life; higher than the Matterhorn and approaching the height of Mont Blanc! She was proud as punch and much improved.

Looking back, one could clearly see how the saddle joined Mawenzi with Kibo. What is not generally understood is that Kilimanjaro is made up of three volcanoes: Shira at 12,300 feet; Mawenzi at 16,700 feet; and, of course, Kibo, the largest and highest, with its summit Uhuru peak.

All our party had arrived and were eating what their upset stomachs would allow and drinking as much as possible to counteract dehydration. We settled in our bunk beds in readiness for sleep, as we had to set off for the summit at 2 a.m. Cathy had now made a complete recovery and was quietly confident. Margaret too, in spite of her nausea, managed to find the situation funny and giggled like a bairn. J.P. and I laughed and exchanged loud banter, which was not really appreciated by Stewart.

"Bloody Hell, you two! How can you feel cheerful on this shit-hole of a mountain. My bloody head is killing me!"

Bob, still smiling, lay on his back looking at the ceiling and murmuring, "Jesus! I hope I can get up!"

Frazer added, "I feel as if I'm bloody dying!"

"You'll be all right, Frazer. Now get some sleep," replied Bob.

With that, we all closed our eyes. The night drifted by and then at the appointed time we were up, clothed, torches on and ready for the fray. The air outside was freezing and this, together with the darkness, was intimidating. Besides us, there were at least sixty people from other groups on the route; German, French and many other languages could be heard.

Nelson, a big Wachagga, was our guide and he seemed to be in a lousy state, with a dreadful cough. Geoff was having a bad time too, having eaten biscuits that were contaminated by paraffin. From the international bunch above us came groans, followed by long bouts of vomiting.

At about 16,500 feet Frazer collapsed, falling heavily on the scree. "Jesus Christ!" he gasped. "I'm finished!"

"Get up, Frazer," urged his dad. "You can do it!"

This made me smile, as Bob himself didn't look too good on his pins. Stewart struggled on in stony silence up the ever steepening slope. Cathy gritted her teeth and I encouraged her.

"Don't think about climbing, just concentrate on your breathing and take small steps. Breathe, Cathy, breathe."

A Frenchman asked me if I would carry his video camera, but I shook my head. Margaret was in hell, sitting down at any opportunity, with J.P. always at hand to help her. Then we noticed that we didn't need torches anymore; the sun's rays heralded the Mummy and Daddy of all dawns.

What an unexpected reward it was for all our efforts to actually experience looking down on the rising sun. With the light and warmth filtering upwards, we felt humbled and rejuvenated. Coleridge's words from "Hymn Before Sunrise" came to me, as we observed Mawenzi's great dark form, silhouetted against the dawn:

> Rise O' ever rise, rise like a cloud of incense from
>   the earth!
> Thou kingly spirit throned among the hills,
> Thou dread ambassador from the earth to heaven,
> Great Hierach! Tell the silent sky,
> And tell the stars, and tell yon rising sun,
> Earth, with her thousand voices, praises God . . .

Time stood still as we sat in quiet meditation, until the gentle voices of the Wachagga guides impressed on us that we still had the hardest part of the climb to do. Sensing our frailty, those noble guides began chanting in their own unique rhythm to help us. "Oh, *Zani-Ko-Ko-Ko*. Oh, *Zani-Ko-Ko-Ko* — Spirit rise up. Spirit rise up." Our tired limbs responded to their rhythm and moved in accord beyond Hans Meyer Cave towards the crater rim.

"About another hundred yards, Cathy, and you've cracked it!" I urged.

I was truly proud of her courage as she ploughed on and on; quite a number of people had packed it in on the final steep slopes and had retired back to the hut. But Cathy, who had been so ill at 14,000 feet, finally placed her feet on the top.

"I feel fine and happy!" she said. "Just a slight humming pain on the side of my head."

Looking around, I could see that all our party had made it, even Frazer. All, that is, except Margaret,

165

who was still gallantly zig-zagging, with J.P. by her side, a little way below. God, she was terribly sick! Then, at last, she made it too, looking frightfully pale and done in.

"Why anyone would even contemplate climbing Mount Everest, God only knows!"

Then Stewart broke his long silence. "I feel shit-awful. Everest? You can stuff it, mate!" With that, he plunged down the scree towards the hut. We all dutifully signed the book and the climb was over.

The descent was colourful and celebratory and within two days we were back at Marangu, thanking Mrs Brice-Bennett and Miss Von Lany for making it all possible.

The following day it was time for farewells. The successful New Zealanders were off home, Margaret and J.P. were to continue their honeymoon further afield in the Dark Continent, and Geoff, Cathy and I were going on safari in the Serengeti.

Bob's smile was bigger than ever before. "I never thought I'd get up, but I did!" he enthused. "And I've got a certificate to prove it!"

Frazer laughed shyly and even Stewart gave us a big smile and admitted that the climb had been worthwhile. The relieved Margaret, glad to be at a comfortable altitude, reluctantly agreed that going high did do something, even if it was only to make you appreciate coming down again! Before you could say "Bob's yer Uncle", amidst waves, shouts and farewells, they were all aboard the open lorry, cruising through the wide gates and out of sight. I felt sad.

Our visit to the Serengeti, which included the Norono Crater and the Oldivi Gorge, the site of Leakey's discovery of earliest man, would require a book in itself to convey its wonders. How comforting to behold a land that is totally unspoilt.

After the safari, brilliantly organised by John Bennett, nephew of Mrs Brice-Bennett, we drove over the border into Kenya and made our way to Nairobi. After a day spent on the Longdot Hills, John took Cathy to Mombasa to see the culture and history of the east coast. Geoff and I rented a jeep, filled it with camping gear and headed for Mount Kenya.

It was interesting to note that, whilst camping in the jungle on the low slopes of the great mountain, elephants had been in close proximity during the night. At 14,000 feet, through a cleft in the rock we entered what seemed like a sanctuary with a green lake, surrounded by soaring mountains and with famous names such as Point John and Point Lenana. We chose the latter, at just over 16,000 feet, which looked a straightforward climb, and ascended it to gain a splendidly close view of Mount Kenya. Unfortunately, our ambition to climb the classic route on that unique mountain, with its twin summits of Batain and Nelion, was thwarted by the weather conditions, and we reluctantly had to trace our way back two hundred miles to Tanzania.

We were on Kilimanjaro again, this time approaching the mountain from Shira Plateau. John Bennett again excelled himself arranging four porters and transport to this remote part of the mountain; I had been bursting at the seams to do a tougher route. This was not easy, as

167

the park warden at the Marangu Gate was most reluctant to allow expeditions on this side of Kilimanjaro. There had been quite a history of people being irresponsible, getting lost and even dying. Rescue was difficult, involving distance, complex terrain and unpredictable weather. It was Bennett's charm and Geoff's credentials that won the day.

Now here we were, camped above Shira's summit at 13,000 feet, with a wild landscape above us leading to the Great Western Breach Wall. In the evening light, the massive Heim and Kirstein glaciers towered above us, filling the sky. We were to ascend the wall by the Arrow Glacier to the crater rim and then move on steep rock to the summit. Both Geoff and I were perfectly acclimatised, the only concern being that Geoff was suffering from a dreadful cold.

That evening a large American party arrived. They were attempting the beautiful and leisurely Unbwe route and we were cordially invited into their huge tent for dinner, a luxury indeed. Their concerns about the altitude and getting up reminded me of our concerns on the tourist route. I earned my supper with my usual story of the 1924 Everest expedition. This had the desired effect and they vowed to climb the mountain in honour of Mallory and Irvine.

The next day, unable to contain my excitement, I motored up towards the Arrow Glacier Hut at 16,000 feet at the base of the Great Wall. The glaciers became larger and larger, filling the landscape until there was barely any sky to see.

Frances, a Wachagga, was the lead guide climber. He

was physically slight and of medium height, with a small beard and dancing eyes. He was incredulous when I sang an African folk song that I remembered hearing Paul Robeson sing in my youth:

Oh! Oh! Oxon and line, river and mountain stream.
Oh! Oh! Oxon and line, we'll come to the water
    hole soon.
I'm not afraid, I'm not afraid, I'm not afraid if my
Shoulders crack, we got to keep going till my
    shoulders crack.
We'll get to that water hole soon . . .
Mighty mountain. Oh, you mighty mountain.
    Mighty mountain . . .

Frances applauded enthusiastically, shouting, "You have a good voice, Simba! You and I climb everything. You no get sick. I know this!"

The strangest thing about Kilimanjaro is its gleaming summit of snow and ice, shining in the hot sun just three degrees south of the equator. About 145 AD, the great Alexandrine astronomer, Ptolemy, wrote of a "Great snow mountain, lying inland from the end of the world". Aristotle too referred to a "So-called Silver Mountain, which might be the source of the Nile". It was to take 1,700 years for the western world to discover Ptolemy's mountain.

Apart from the occasional mention of "The Egyptian Mount Olympus", west of Mombasa, nothing was known about Kilimanjaro until two missionaries, Krapf and Rebmann, set eyes on it in 1847. It was first ascended by a German, Hans Meyer, and his alpine guide, Ludwig Purtscheller, in 1889. Their ascent was a good deal harder than it is now, because the glaciers are receding and, at that time, the ice was far more treacherous to cross.

At last we arrived at the Arrow Glacier Hut. The porters elected to camp inside, while Geoff and I erected our small tent. To my right I could see the intimidating Breach Wall that Messner had climbed years before.

It snowed heavily during the night, and at 2 a.m., the porters shook the dusty white covering off our tent and provided us with large mugs of tea. It was time to go. The snow had ceased by this time and we could just make out the Arrow Glacier's ghost-like form through the darkness.

Headlamps were on and the first steps taken. Three of the porters had decided not to go any further as they were sick. Our party was now reduced to Frances, Geoff and Yours Truly. Although I was acclimatised, the effort of climbing up frozen scree made my heart beat violently and, as the scree gave way to rocks, it was a relief to be able to use my arms again. I was surprised to find how steep it was and grateful that it was technically easy.

After a while Geoff said, "You can turn your head torch off. It's light!"

I had not noticed. I was so intent on getting up.

I took a short rest and absorbed our surroundings. On my immediate right was the huge Heim Glacier, its vast ridges containing frozen, hanging cataracts of snow, sweeping majestically down towards the plateau. I had driven Geoff mad with my requests to climb it. Finally, in no uncertain terms, he had said "No": we hadn't the time, the climb was dangerous and long and it required a great deal of organisation and back-up. Reluctantly, I bowed to his knowledge and experience. When I tentatively mentioned the Kirstein Glacier, which was now on our far left, his pained face said all and he shook his head.

Nevertheless, our route was a good one, skirting the side of the Arrow Glacier, so called because it looks like an arrow head, and heading in a straight line for the crater rim. At about 17,500 feet, Geoff announced that he was going down. I was actually surprised that he had got that far. His lousy cold was getting much, much worse, no joke at these altitudes, and complications can develop so easily.

"Shall I come down with you?" I asked.

"No!" he replied vehemently. "Keep going and try and complete the climb. And watch how you go!"

It was sad watching Geoff go down; we were very close and he always made mountaineering seem less intimidating to me. Now there was nothing for it but to continue with my faithful guide, Frances. His non-stop cheerful banter and requests for me to sing more songs made me forget our predicament. It is fair to say that, although he knew the mountain well, he was no Joe Brown!

We encountered a thin mist at 18,500 feet and he seemed to lose his way a little. He veered right onto some rotten, unstable rock. But when I asked, he charmingly agreed to allow me to take the lead for a while. I chose a more vertical and strenuous route, but one which was on firmer and more stable rock. Two well protected chimneys caught my eye, which seemed to lead to easy ground at the top of the wall. My assessment, thank goodness, proved correct and, on completing these pitches, Frances again happily took the lead.

After a few minor hiccups, we were on top of the rim, looking down into a fantastic, desert-like crater. The time was about 8 a.m. and we sat down for breakfast.

"You go well, Simba. You no sick?" Frances enquired.

"No," I replied.

"Dat is good. Now we go everywhere. First, Ruesh Crater, then round and round to the top of mountain. Yes?"

"I try, Frances. I try," I nodded.

I was wonderfully happy. It was exhilarating and surprising to be in a landscape that bore a resemblance to the terrain found on Mars that I had stared at so often in my books at home. The pinkish-beige desert region stretched out for miles in every direction, rising here and there in great sandy dunes. Astonishingly, great ice cliffs protruded out incongruously amidst this sea of sand.

On my right was the Furtwangler Glacier, positively vibrating in the sun, with intricate colours of green, blue, pink and white. What phenomenal architectural mind conjured up this vision? One could understand why the legendary leopard, made famous by Hemingway in *The Snows of Kilimanjaro*, had made its final resting place here. Leopard's Point, where the body was discovered in 1926 by D. V. Latham, was further round, near the Ratzel Glacier. When I asked why the leopard had come to such a height, Frances quietly answered, "It was becoming a man."

It would seem that Kilimanjaro has always drawn animals to its summit. Elephant remains have been found on the slopes at 15,000 feet. African wild dogs have been seen on the summit.

Much refreshed, Frances and I headed straight across the sand to a distant hill, from which I could look into the Reush Crater. A legend tells of King Menelik I, son of King Solomon and the Queen of Sheba, who camped on the saddle below Kibo on his way home from conquering East Africa. That night he felt death approaching, so he took all his servants and treasure up to the Kibo crater and disappeared into it. It is said that an offspring of his family will return one day, find a ring that was on Menelik's finger and this great seal ring will give him the wisdom and power of Solomon.

On arriving at the Ruesh Crater, I looked down. Down it went, God knows how many feet. The colossal round rim seemed to go on for miles and the wind tore round and round its primitive ramparts, roaring its triumphant call: "This is the heart of Kilimanjaro! I am Kibo, the Good One; the chastiser of Mawenzi, the Evil One; the gentle caresser of ancient Shira."

The name Mawenzi means "The Jagged One". The word Kibo means spotted or piebald and is thought to refer to the appearance of the peak with its dark black rocks, spotted and streaked by the tongues of the summit glaciers. My eyes penetrated deeper to the floor of the crater, where fumaroles and sulphur deposits, surrounded by small blue flowers, could be seen. Kibo is still active, ever watchful of Mawenzi's behaviour.

The summit was now the objective and we moved down the valley towards it. Beneath an overhanging ice wall, we came across the carcass of an African wild dog. This was at about 19,000 feet.

"Is he becoming a man too?" I asked Frances.

"No, Simba. He just wants peace."

I was going directly up the black cliffs, via Furtwangler Point, into an easy snow gully and on to the big easy rocks. Frances shook his head vigorously, pointing the way by a long winding route to the left. "Much easier, much better, Simba." He smiled.

Again, I nodded to my better and, in perfect harmony, we moved over shallow snow and easy rock to the pathway leading to the summit. The wind dropped, ushering in a stillness that soothed my overstretched senses. Higher and higher. I placed one foot after the other as, far below me, the sea of clouds stretched unendingly beyond the horizon. It was as if I were on a colossal rock, floating in a vast heaven above the brilliant azure of the sky.

The rarefied atmosphere, containing half the oxygen at sea level, had the effect of gently popping open unseen chambers in my brain. It was sensuous and musical and I channelled this delicate joy to unused levels of consciousness, all new to me, yet strangely familiar.

A few more steps, just a few, and I was there at the summit, embracing that noble Wachagga, Frances, in my arms. Uhuru Peak; Freedom Peak; Ptolemy's "Great snow mountain". We sat there together, still and silent, and words from Genesis came to mind:

"And he dreamed, and beheld a ladder set upon the earth, and the top of it reached to Heaven; and beheld the angels of God ascending and descending on it."

Our descent was fast and there to greet me, with love and a huge mug of tea, was Geoff. He was thrilled to bits; what an unselfish, generous soul. The African adventure was over.

CHAPTER
TEN

The Toy Train

This chapter is about my rendezvous and momentous meeting with a smoking, steaming little dragon, or, to put it more prosaically, my journey in 1990 aboard the Toy Train that travels from Siliguri to Darjeeling in India, that mysterious and fascinating country. The mere thought of this small locomotive with a huge heart, throws aside the very frontiers of time itself, and shunts one willingly backwards as though aboard H. G. Wells's time machine to days of childhood and bliss.

You must have gathered by now that I am a veritable Peter Pan and quite incapable of ever growing up. I am but a child, and nobut more! My childhood was so blissfully happy that even today the same jolly DNA molecules of my infancy dance about together with a frolicsome fizz! Out of this bubbly jamboree of flotsam explode memories of the 1940s BBC radio programmes such as "Dick Barton — Special Agent"; "The Man in Black"; "ITMA"; "Happydrome" and "Saturday Night Theatre". My oh my! The remembrance of it all makes me want to jump up and down and filch a lollipop from the fridge! "Paul Temple"! We were thrilled by episodes, and transported to distant horizons by the magic of the music that introduced each episode. Yes! "Coronation Scot". Oh, the steady beat of the orchestra as the train got up steam and then relaxed into its insistent rhythm. Trains, trains, trains; we all loved 'em. In those early years, they were a main topic of conversation morning, noon and night, filling our minds' eyes with visions of their colossal bodies, power and energy.

My home at the time was 30, Probert Avenue, Goldthorpe, near Rotherham, Yorkshire. The street was part of a circle containing a hundred houses or more. On opposite sides ran two railway lines: one was rusty and disused, but the other was part of the Great North Eastern Railway. On many a summer's afternoon I would sit at the back of a neighbour's house which overlooked the LNER railway line, watching the smoking engines go by. Goods trains would struggle with all their might to pull the iron wagons loaded with ore, and one rainy day a train seemed almost to buckle its metal wheels and pulleys as it groaned with the effort of its task. Sparks flew as the wheels ran free, unable to grip the wet track, and the sweating stokers, lit up by the boiler, shovelled coal at an incredible rate in an attempt to sustain the engine. The roar of the frustrated train and the massive eruptions of grey-black smoke from the funnel were reminiscent of some belaboured dragon and inspired me to cheer them to the rooftops for their magnificent effort. The grimy face of the driver smiled broadly as he raised his LNER hat in thanks and sounded his shrill whistle.

Moments like these were memorable, but nothing

compared to the sight of the great express trains. Racing and pulsating across the countryside, these giants of iron and steel with their fiery bellies of burning coal sent shivers of pride through the hearts of all who beheld them. What names they had! Names that blazed out and bethumped the senses. Names of mystery and legend! Names that caressed the heart and mind and lit the way to visions of misty dawns, red sunsets, and promises of far off and untold delights!

Green Arrow, Golden Arrow, Devon Belle, Duke of Gloucester, Osprey, Princess Elizabeth, King Edward, Lord Nelson, Capitals Limited, Queen of Scots, Royal Scot, Black Bull, Cheltenham Flyer, Hush Hush, Galloping Alice, and King Arthur of Southern Railways; not forgetting, of course, the pride of Wales, the magnificent Red Dragon, or the much loved ugly duckling of the south east, the bullied Q1-0-6-0S class power train, the Bournemouth Belle. As it approached the gentle sea resort of Eastbourne, the sound of its unmistakable deep exhausts forced admiring smiles from the reserved inhabitants and gladdened their hearts.

Now, I hear you shout and complain that I have missed out this train and that. Forgive me. How can a simple lad like myself cover such a vast tapestry of steaming delight? Forgive me if I merely scratch the tenders of these immortals. What of Scotland, for instance? Indeed! Scotland's voice was lyrical and loud in the early 1930s, demanding a train to challenge its fierce slopes. In response, in May 1934 the famous Plant Works in Doncaster produced the monstrous class P No. 2000, Cock of the North. It was a massive engine, seventy-three feet and eight inches in length, with eight coupled wheels of six feet two inches in diameter, to give the necessary adhesion when climbing steep gradients. Scotland was proud and satisfied that at last a mighty locomotive had been created that was worthy of its countryside, and the Highlands rejoiced in their new-found friend.

At this time, more than 20,000 route miles of track bore the weight of these steaming metal giants as they sped through every nook and cranny of the British Isles. "Look! A train's coming!" people would shout, and then run to any convenient spot to wave passionately at the passing train, exhilarated by an inexplicable feeling of *joie de vivre*.

During the wild windy spring days of the late Forties, youngsters like myself, with runny noses and streaming eyes, would gather at the aforementioned Doncaster Plant Works. Here we collected as many train numbers as possible and heard whispered tales of an apple-green train that defied description and stupefied the mind. So deeply passionate were the feelings this locomotive engendered, that people who had observed it became weirdly incoherent, their staring eyes suggesting that their hearts and minds had been enslaved and spirited far away to be forever conjoined with that sacred express.

In moments of fleeting lucidity they managed to press a forefinger to their lips and in hushed silence stammer the name, "The Flying Scotsman".

"It is the most stupendous train ever created."

"Amazing!"

"Stunning!"

"Breathtaking!"

"Gigantic!"

"When it thunders past you, the whole railway embankment shakes beneath yer feet. Hundreds of sparks fly up from its wheels and set bushes on fire! If you stand too close, it'll blast yer off yer feet."

"There's nowt like it for elegant ferocity."

In this charged atmosphere a brave lad called Malcolm, only eleven years of age, quietly suggested that the Southern's prestigious Victoria–Dover Marina Boat Train, The Golden Arrow, was as good as The Flying Scotsman, any day. He barely escaped a lynching. After a very long and terrifying pause, he was bombarded with a barrage of deafening expletives from the throng of indignant lads, myself included.

Malcolm gallantly stood his ground, and repeated his assertion, the effort turning his pink complexion puce, which fused comically with his red hair. As the tirade of abuse grew louder, and little Malcolm was surrounded by hostile boys, a hail of female voices silenced all and everyone.

"Watch yer pit language, and leave the lad alone, yer great bullies, he's perfectly entitled to his own opinion. The lad's right. There are other trains besides The Flying Scotsman, yer know."

These words came from a large group of women who worked at the plant. Immediately, we sucked in air and held our breaths, at the same time lowering our heads in shame and removing our LNER caps in deep respect for our attractive chastisers. All conflict quickly evaporated as they wandered amongst us, ruffling our hair with friendly fingers and adopting pugilistic stances in readiness to "box our ears off". This good-natured ribaldry restored our good senses, and Malcolm's arm was in danger of being shaken off as we vigorously offered our apologies.

Much to the amusement of the ladies, a chubby lad called Carlin announced he had a cigarette card of "The Golden Arrow" at home, and would Malcolm care to swop? Two steel ball-bearings and five clay marbles were immediately offered by our red-faced companion, and Carlin happily concluded the deal, to everyone's delight. The ladies then enthralled us with mesmerising tales of the Great Trains. Our admiration for their knowledge knew no bounds, as they had helped build and repair hundreds of steaming dragons.

I was acquainted with one of them, a dark-eyed, pretty young lass of eighteen with a never-ending smile called Betty Sutcliffe. She worked the day shift at the plant from 6 a.m. to 6 p.m. — a full twelve hours! Although I was only twelve years old, we had a lot in common and got on famously. She earned between £300 and £400 a year, depending on how much overtime she put in. Like several of the other ladies, she had attended a one-year engineering course in Sheffield, and was classified as a fully skilled worker.

On the occasional Saturday morning, several of us lads would be allowed into the heart of the plant to observe the ladies at work. They were tremendous! With devastating efficiency they beetled about at a rate of knots, cleaning axle boxes, repairing engine lubricating systems and making rivet bolts on capstan lathes. Despite the noise level, their laughter and chit-chat could clearly be heard above the machines, filling every nook and cranny of the plant.

The most impressive sight of all was a handsome young lady driving a ten-ton crane with consummate ease and lifting enormous sheets of steel over iron rollers, ready for shaping into boilers. Gradually, piece by piece, from tiny rivets to great sheets of steel and tubing, we began to discern the outline and then, finally, the birth of the trains. It was sheer magic.

Out of a work force of 585, 183 were women. They fell into three categories: skilled, semi-skilled and unskilled. Most of them wore the official green boiler suit, though overalls were much in evidence. They also generally wore hats, if not, their hair was tied back severely to prevent it tangling with the machinery. They were also employed in the car locomotive shed, carriage shops, boiler shop, iron foundry, paint shop and stores. It was the ladies who cared for the carriages, varnishing them inside and out, painstakingly mending upholstery and washing down dirty carriages. Their forearms reminded me of Popeye's after eating spinach!

In 1953 the plant held its Centenary celebrations. I remember the joyful day very well. Five hundred people joined in a celebratory excursion from Doncaster to King's Cross and back. On the outward journey, the pilot engine was the first small Atlantic train. No. 990, Henry Oakley; the return journey was made with that train behind the great Gresley Pacific locomotive, No. 60014, Silver Link. Two new names to ponder there, my avid readers: "Gresley" and "Silver Link".

Ah, Gresley! Sir Nigel Gresley! A knight errant, if ever there was one, appointed by the LNER as chief mechanical engineer as early as 1923. Tall of stature, with wavy, well-groomed hair, solidly dressed in a heavy tweed suit, with a waistcoat sporting a watch and chain, and, of course, a pipe, he was to prove an outstanding influence in the railway industry for generations. He gazed out on Europe and homed in with beady eyes on the Italian racing car manufacturer and pioneer in stream-lining, Ettore Bugatti. The combined talent of these two luminaries resulted in the LNER agreeing to the construction at Doncaster of a train with the Bugatti wedge-shaped front.

You can see where I'm leading you, can't you? Aye! To the smashing A4 Pacific locomotives! Oh, I faint! I quiver! I shake! My oh my! The great Pacifics displayed a variety of colours from black, silver, grey, blue, green right through to vibrant red. Thirty-five of them were built at the plant, from Silver Link 2509 to the last, Peregrine 4903, and they were the most successful Pacifics ever built. How do I know? Because, mate, I, Brian Blessed, was there! There to see an express that tore out my innards and satisfied every mad craving in my imagination. I am, of course, referring to the Pacific A4, Mallard.

Half a dozen times I saw it in Doncaster, and on each occasion fell to my knees in supplication. I saw it bursting through smog and rain, its colossal, blue Bugatti wedge-shaped front powering through dense air and spraying massive jets of water from the drenched track onto awestruck static tenders. All the while, the begrimed faces of the driver and the stokers seemed suspended in a mist of volcanic red, as their proud wild eyes opened and shut in time with the rhythm of the rampant gigantic pistons. The devastating Leviathan drove on like a blue Moby Dick, defying elements of earth and sky, and from its fiery belly roared out a challenge to space itself. It is recorded that on 3 July 1938, the Pacific A4 Mallard achieved a top speed of 126 MPH on a test run down Stoke Bank, breaking the world speed record for a steam locomotive.

In the late 1950s the great steam locomotives continued to grace our lines. The Class 7P Britannia and Oliver Cromwell, each weighing ninety-four tons, were frequently seen, as was Class 8P Duke of Gloucester. The much loved Green Knight Class 4MT, sixty-seven point nine tons, had made its debut for East Somerset Railways, and the steam engines' survival, it seemed, was assured for the foreseeable future by the planned introduction of the Class 9F series, which included Morning Star and the impressive Black Prince.

In fact, nothing could have been further from the truth. We had been lulled into a false sense of security, and the bleak wind of change was about to blow across the land. The appearance of the much publicised Beeching Plan aroused great concern amongst those who considered the retention of an extensive railway network an essential component of a well-balanced transport system. The closure proposed in 1963, of 5,000 out of 21,000 route miles of line and 2363 out of 7000 stations, was mostly completed by 1967.

During the summer of that year, I sat on an

embankment in Goldthorpe with my young brother Alan, and watched sadly as the locomotives went by for the last time. We were devastated. The aptly named train, the Evening Star, of the 9F series heralded the beginning of the end. From far and wide, the powers that be gave orders for all trains to report to various scrapyards throughout the British Isles. It was a holocaust of epic proportions. In these scrapyards, like the ones at Drapers in Hull and Carnforth in Wales, the last knockings took place and the dying commenced. Like whales beached on distant shores or elephants trumpeting from their secret burial grounds, the trains moaned and groaned and fought to stay alive in their static positions until their last courageous breaths hissed out from unyielding pistons and their great hearts ceased to beat.

In August 1968, British Rail dropped the fires for the last time and the age of steam was over. But, as if in answer to a nation's prayer, preservationists appeared from the four corners of the kingdom and made heroic efforts to save some of the trains. Ninety per cent were destroyed (except their furnaces which were made out of copper), but miraculously 260 were spared. The Keighley and Worth Valley Railway had a negotiator of proven ability in the late Ron Ainsworth, who saved many trains; the splendid Peter Beet and his colleagues at Carnforth also performed wonders. Drapers' scrapyard itself nobly preserved such locomotives as the Stanier 5MT 45305. This train is maintained today by the Humberside Locomotive Preservation Group. Several companies were set up at the time, such as the

Bluebell Railway. Because of their efforts the golden age of steam is preserved today.

British Rail's asking price for any locomotive in 1968 was £3,500, or three for £9,000. Just think, you could have bought The Flying Scotsman for £3,500! As for the Mallard, it can be seen today at the National Train Museum in the historic city of York. What better setting could it have? There it stands: powerful, massive, streamlined, elegant and pristine in vibrant blue. All trains seem to have faces, and the Mallard with its Bugatti wedge-shaped front looks pugnacious yet friendly and refined. Its whole appearance suggests that it is ever ready to power out of the museum and burst its cylinders once again.

Today there are three million members of preservation societies throughout Britain, and steam trains continue to prosper and thrive throughout the world: Pakistan; Zimbabwe; South Africa; Russia — you name the country and the steaming dragons are frequently there. Which brings me to the star of my story — the Toy Train.

Follow me now, my patient readers, as I guide you through the morning mists of India with its shimmering tracks and hot steaming engines to the foothills of the Himalayas, and finally, at last, to the Toy Train.

In the autumn of 1989, two years after returning from the snows of Kilimanjaro, our impossible dream of mounting a film about the 1924 expedition to Everest became a reality. Charging with his lance on all fronts, my Sir Galahad, John-Paul Davidson, had miraculously managed to persuade the good old BBC to provide half of the budget. The remaining money had been enthusiastically drummed up by a dashing cavalier of a producer, Stephen Evans. Stephen was known affectionately to his friends as Taffy, but I called him Sir Taffy, an apt title, for if Davidson's Galahad armour was black, then Evans's was rusty and blood-stained from his knightly exploits on the battlefield at Agincourt. Sir Taffy, you see, had been instrumental in finding the "pot of gold at the end of the rainbow" which enabled Kenneth Branagh to make his inspirational film of Shakespeare's *Henry V*.

Now with these two knights behind me the Everest expedition and film were finally secured.

It had taken twenty years to mount the Everest film, twenty years of expectation, frustration, hope and despair. Now, at last, we had won through, and the joy was intoxicating. Day in, day out, my heart throbbed uncontrollably. Happiness galloped through my being and made sleep remote and unobtainable.

Heady days indeed! The words of the ancient Greeks came to mind — "Beware, if you want something hard enough, you may get it" — for monstrous challenges lay ahead and all would depend on my fitness. My only answer to this excitement and trepidation was to gather up my army of canines and race madly over Chobham Common until my lungs were bursting and my legs would carry me no more. If anyone had witnessed these jaunts with the dogs they would have thought me unbalanced, for I would chatter and laugh, break into song and jig about like a jack-in-a-box. "God in Heaven!" I would roar. "Thank you!"

Once, on the hilltop overlooking the common, with model aircraft flying and buzzing around me, I lay on my back panting, the dogs nestled alongside me, licking my ears. As my energies subsided into a sublime stillness, with Surrey's gentle heath cushioning my body, I dreamed of Everest, thousands of miles away. The snows would be heavy there now, I thought, yet soon the west wind would blow and, with the warming of the spring and with luck, we would scale its flanks.

Forgive me if I now discontinue the account of the Everest Expedition, as I have covered the whole epic in my book *The Turquoise Mountain*. It's time to return to the subject of this chapter: steam engines.

Part of our great adventure was to film the Toy Train that had transported the Everestiers of the Twenties from Siliguri to Darjeeling. I admit that, at the time, the thought of travelling on that marvellous little "Chuffa Billy" excited me almost as much as going to Everest itself.

In the spring of 1990, I arrived by plane in Bagdogora, India, with a BBC film team which included J.P., the director; Margaret; a three-man BBC crew and a young lady called Shenni Italia, who was our Indian fixer from the expedition's Delhi office. From Bagdogora we journeyed by bus and after some considerable time arrived at Siliguri. This beetling town is captivating: it has the same energy as Calcutta but none of its traffic. The dusty streets ring to the sound of trishaws, which have three wheels the size of ordinary bicycle wheels and a carriage attached to the back which will carry up to three people. How quiet and clean it would be if these were used in the country lanes of Britain!

The shops seduced both J.P. and myself, reminding me of those I had known as a small boy during the war. There was a cobbler, a little grocery shop and an old-fashioned barber. The influence of the British Raj was everywhere to be seen. I eagerly bought my father a packet of filter-tipped Gold Flake cigarettes that must have been sitting there for years!

Eventually we left the shops and dimly lit tea-rooms, for now, at last, it was time to see the legendary Toy Train. At that moment I was six again and remembered my Dad putting the finishing touches to my Hornby train set, with its circular track which ran around the table and chairs of our sitting room.

Now, right in front of me, was a slightly larger version, a proper beauty with a compact blue body, lots of steam and smoke and a piercing whistle. I wanted to climb on board there and then, but there were wretched forms to complete, so J.P. and I entered a tiny room, where Margaret and Shenni were making the necessary arrangements with the station master. We kept well out of the way, and sat on a table at the far end of the room, with our legs dangling down, grinning from ear to ear and sucking sherbets.

"Just look at them," said Margaret. "A pair of naughty little boys."

A moment later we were off. Shenni was with me on the train; J.P., Margaret and the crew following alongside in a large van, filming. Steam poured out, and the pistons worked nineteen to the dozen, pumping out their energetic song. The song, it seemed to me, was the song the school children sang who travelled from Siliguri to Darjeeling:

> "Down from Old Mount Herman on the small Toy
>   Train,
> after nine months' mugging, back home again,
> teachers are so rosy, children are the same,
> everyone is happy, waiting for the train.
>
> Ghoom, Sonada, Kurselong, are all left behind,
> though the journey's very long, I'm sure we do
>   not mind,
> when we reach Sealdah, hail it with a shout,
> Pan Beeri cigarette, hop the bloomy out!"

"This journey can go on for ever as far as I am concerned," I shouted out.

It was, in fact, to take the best part of a day, as it was fifty miles from Siliguri to Darjeeling, and an ascent of 8,000 feet. The train would stop frequently for a well-earned drink, but, once replenished, it would take a deep breath, suck up heat from its well-stoked furnace and power on again cheerfully.

This dear little train is also called "The Crook-a-dest Train in the World" and with good reason, as up and up we went, turning and twisting and shunting backwards and forwards. It made figures of eight, zig-zags and loops, and once the engine passed the tail of the train and the driver exchanged pleasantries with the passengers in the last coach!

"Can you get up on the roof?" shouted J.P. from the van, which either kept alongside us or raced ahead for some spiffing shot.

"Yes, of course I can," and in a flash I was up on the top with a concerned Shenni shouting warnings from below.

An official followed me like a demented Gunga Din. "Please sir! No sir! You must be careful sir!"

I calmed him with a confident smile, and cooed at the spectacular scenery around me: great plunging cliffs and deep green valleys. We passed the Terai whose jungles were still the home of the tiger. Oh my, oh my. It was time to have a boiled egg and a sandwich, and I chomped away contentedly, like a baby in a pram.

An old ditty from my school days buzzed in my brain:

"The train goes running along the line,
Jicketi can, jicketi can!
I wish it were mine, I wish it were mine!
Jicketi can, jicketi can!
The engine driver stands in front,
He makes it run, he makes it shunt.
Down from the downs, down from the downs,
Up to the towns, up to the towns,
Down the ridges and over the lea,
Down the ledges and up to the sea,
With a jicketi can, jicketi can — whoowa Hoooo."

Whoowa Hooo! went the whistle of the Toy Train to herald our arrival at Ghoom. Then, on again, with other words from my childhood surfacing: "Faster than fairies, faster than witches, bridges, houses, hedges and ditches . . ."

"Can you stand on the roof, Brian?" roared J.P. "Look over here — that's great! Now we're coming aboard for close-ups."

There I'd been, standing just like Mallory when Captain Noel filmed him in 1922. This was smashing! Better than anything on earth! You could run right round the moon and it wouldn't be as good as this!

As the train stopped briefly, the crew joined me, breathless and jolly. "Brian," laughed J.P. "You looked like a little boy! You never stopped grinning!"

I made a big effort to be serious, but it was all in vain. Giggling and grinning, I hummed "Pasadena" and remained identified with my childhood. But, if I was six years old, the film crew were barely six and a half, for their behaviour was easily as juvenile as my own.

We resumed our journey and as a low bridge presented itself my Indian minder shouted, "Down please! Down!" Smoke from the funnel enveloped me and filled my nostrils with that unique aroma. My face was as black as soot.

We had been growing impatient to see the promised vision of the mighty mountain Kanchenjunga at the end of our journey but, instead, on arriving at Darjeeling we were greeted by a dark grey sky and wet mist; weather that was much more suited to Manchester. Our heroic train, whistling with pride, its smoke and steam mingling with the mist around us, came to a pulsating stop.

For the last twenty minutes I had been up front with

the two drivers helping shovel coal into the furnace. Now I patted the Toy Train, thanking it for making a dream come true. The age of steam will never die, whilst such a train exists. You couldn't help but be moved by its pugnacious performance.

Contentedly, we made our way through the dark, damp streets of Darjeeling, towards the inviting warmth of the famous Windermere Hotel. This hotel had been built during the Twenties for visiting tea planters and special guests. It was done in true colonial style, with white bricks and green corrugated roofs topped with graceful white chimney pots. There was a large veranda, with tables and chairs under pretty coloured sun-shades, overlooking a dense green valley.

That evening a fire burned merrily in my room which had been provided by a small Sikkinese gentleman for five rupees. As I lay in my bed as warm as toast, watching the flames growing smaller and flickering out, my thoughts turned once again to the Toy Train. A mile down the road, in a warm, quiet shunting shed, it too had turned in for the night and was sweetly yawning, closing its eyes and enjoying its well-earned rest.

"Oh, gracious, little steam train," I murmured, "are you aware that over 5,000 miles away, in the National Railway Museum in York, you have a big brother? He too sleeps in a large hall; powerful, massive, streamlined, elegant and pristine in vibrant blue; ever ready to power out of the museum, to burst his cylinders once again, to please all and, hopefully, to meet you?"

CHAPTER
ELEVEN

The Laughing Lama
of Dharamsala

"Tread softly, for this is holy ground
it may be, could we look with seeing eyes
this spot we stand upon is paradise."

Christina Rossetti

One day, in the autumn of 1990, I arrived at Delhi Airport in India, breathlessly awaiting the official nod to commence my next adventure. A tall, middle-aged, turbaned inspector with hawk-like features scrupulously perused my baggage and papers. After what seemed like an interminable amount of time, he emitted a forlorn sigh and reluctantly allowed me to pass through onto the baking hot tarmac and the awaiting internal aircraft.

Shielding my eyes from the blazing sun, I saw in the distance lush foliage, water buffaloes and large still ponds laced with vibrant red lilies. The enchantment of it all drew me away from the direct path to the plane and I was gently chastised by a jolly official for getting out of line. Immediately I nodded an apology and with a smile added, "Oh, India! Even from here it looks mysterious and inviting."

"Yes, Sir," responded the official. "India always magical! Once it touches your heart, Sir, you will never be the same."

Happy, happy Brian! I cooed to myself, as I clambered aboard the tiny Vyadoot Airways twin-engined Pilantus plane, bound for sacred places and exotic delights. As is my wont in such circumstances, the child in me burst forth and the emotion of the moment danced giddily up my spine and plucked a musical chord in my Adam's Apple. Out came the song: "We're off to see the Wizard, the wonderful Wizard of Oz!" In all their travels in that land of Munchkins and witches, I doubt if Dorothy, Scarecrow, Tin Man and Cowardly Lion felt excitement that exceeded ours!

I say ours, for I was sharing this latest adventure with my three trusty Musketeers, "all for one and one for all": J.P. whom you all know by now, David Breashears, the world famous climber and film-maker, and his bride to be, explorer and trainee camera lady, Veronique Choa. Veronique is a beautiful, young, dark-haired American, with high cheek bones and oriental features. David is in his early thirties and is also an American. Dark-haired and handsome, he exuded fitness, as befits a mountaineer, tall, slim and raw boned. It was almost impossible to decipher the colour of his eyes, as they seemed now green, now blue, now grey and mysterious and exciting like a pair of prisms.

A few months earlier, in the spring of that year, the four of us had shared storms, extreme cold and blistering heat on the northern side of Mount Everest in Tibet. There we had finally realised our dream and made our film about the exploits of George Leigh Mallory and his magnificent companions on that towering mountain in the early Twenties.

J.P. and a BBC team had performed brilliantly, filming up to 22,000 feet. From that point on, Veronique, David and a young BBC soundman named Graham Hoyland, two Sherpas named Chuldim and Nawang, and myself, reached a point at about 26,000 feet on the North Ridge of Everest and completed the filming — with the exception of one very important sequence. This was the sequence which we were now about to embark on, one of very special significance to Yours Truly.

The gathering excitement of it all increased with the rhythm and energy of the plane's propellers and once more I repeated to myself the words, "We're off to see the Wizard," which forced J.P. to admonish me sweetly and say, "No Brian! You must not call him a wizard."

David echoed J.P.'s sentiments and, doubled over with mirth at the thought of this meeting, added, "I wonder what he will make of Brian?"

The wizard to whom I was referring did not reside in the Emerald City at all; in fact, of course, he was not a wizard! The divine gentleman I was singing about had once lived under the golden roofs of the impressive gigantic Potala Palace of Lhasa, in the ancient land of Bo, known today as Tibet. Now he lives in Dharamsala in India, a village which is affectionately known as "Little Lhasa". I am, of course, referring to His Holiness, the fourteenth Dalai Lama, Tenzin Gyatso.

The BBC had arranged for me to be blessed by His Holiness a few months earlier, in April, prior to going to Everest. The meeting and blessing was to be filmed. It related historically to a meeting in 1920 between the thirteenth Dalai Lama and Sir Charles Bell, CIE, the British political officer for Tibetan affairs. Sir Charles was one of the few men to have won the confidence and friendship of the thirteenth Dalai Lama. He received an invitation to visit Lhasa, the sacred city, in 1920 and stayed there for one year. Eventually, he obtained permission for the British to go to Tibet to explore and possibly climb Mount Everest in 1921.

Unfortunately, our 1990 BBC expedition got bogged down in Bhutan in April and we missed our audience with His Holiness. I was devastated. Nevertheless, the Dalai Lama did send me his prayers and it is no exaggeration to say that I certainly felt them on the mountain.

Now His Holiness had kindly agreed to try a second time to help us complete our film. He would perform the ceremony and give me his blessing. This blessing would serve a double purpose, relating both to the 1990 Everest expedition and to my next one, which would take place in 1993. My previous disappointment was forgotten, for now, at last, I would meet His Holiness.

Our noisy, vibrating aircraft was capable of holding only about a dozen passengers, and we felt rather like sardines in a tin. But what fun! As the cabin was not pressurized, we flew at a height of about 2,000 feet and consequently experienced a delightful intimacy with the earth below us. Could not the Emerald City itself be down there? It was not an idle question for, as far as the eye could see, were miles and miles of emerald forest; green mansions of ethereal delight which drank in the sun's rays and reflected back their ultra-violet power from trillions of leaves, that danced in celebration of the cosmic dancer himself, All Glories, Shiva, known sometimes as Nataraja, whose dance shook the cosmos and created the world.

Dance, dance, dance, my mind swooned to the rhythm of Nataraja. Our Pilantus Pegasus seemed to capture the mood and rolled and turned effortlessly along gorges and above streams, almost caressing the tree tops and inspiring a mixed flock of birds to join in the frolic. On and on, until on the shimmering horizon we discerned the purple and gold foothills of the Himalayas.

My eyes again peered downwards to penetrate and try to solve the mysteries of the forest. The rapid journey of the afternoon sun, in company with the gradual build-up of altocumulus clouds, created sudden darts of light that revealed unexpected shades of vegetation and half-hidden glades. Yet, the jungle possessively hid all from my gaze. Within its rampant growth I knew there were gentle feathered stems that supported parnassias, swertias, sweet-scented pink orchids and fritillaria of many kinds. In the overwhelming push for light were magnolias, bamboos, alders, sycamores, all draped with long bearded wisps of lichen. Though the monsoon was not yet at an end, the result of its life-giving rains was evident everywhere. The rays of the sun kissed and sucked the moisture skywards and the resulting humidity no doubt drew the writhing leeches forth, to drop insidiously from overhanging juniper trees on unsuspecting passersby, to gorge on their blood.

Yes, the jungle hid all. A million creatures in India within a hair's breadth of mankind's touch, zealously camouflage themselves from our gaze and trust not the negative part of our nature. They run, run, like Rudyard Kipling's Red Dogs, following their instinct and heeding only the call and songs of the Blue Clad Lord, Krishna, and the pulse of the wild.

As I pressed my face against the window of the plane to take in another tantalising piece of scenery, my thoughts remained with Kipling. His very soul seems to embrace an extraordinary reality that one cannot help but be fascinated by. The strange combination of the British and the Indian amusingly defies analysis, but "back home" you can always spot those English families whose roots are deeply planted in India. Kipling is a fine example of the mystique. I dearly love his creation of *The Jungle Book* and the adventures of Mowgli. There have been many tales in India of babies being suckled and brought up by wolves. As our plane throttled back and prepared to land at the half-way point of our journey, I relaxed in my seat, closed my eyes and dreamt of dry warm caves and snuggling naked human infants, greedily drinking from the nipples of proud mother wolves.

Once more my nose pressed against the window, as the plane started its fast descent. Could Mowgli the Elephant Boy exist down there? I mused. "Of course he could!" I almost shouted back. So indeed could Sheer Khan, the tiger; Bagheera, the black panther; and all the other colourful creatures in the story — not forgetting of course the "honk-honk" sound of Kaa, the huge reticulated python. All would be rejoicing in a jungle that contained secrets, pale pavilions, long-lost temples of Vishnu, the presenter, and vine-encrusted golden statues of Ganesh, the elephant-headed god of prosperity and wisdom.

We landed with a bump outside the town of Chandigar, a place of round roads and bright beige buildings, designed by the celebrated French architect Corbusier. A few people disembarked and others replaced them, while we remained patiently in our seats. I was glad of this because the place was crawling with soldiers in green uniforms, each carrying what looked like some sort of black Sten gun. The sight was disappointing and depressing, and seemed out of place amidst the trees and flowers.

The soldiers were proud and arrogant, occasionally cocking their weapons in the air, as if to blast some imaginary eagle from the sky. How impotent they looked, how wretched! If a painter had been commissioned to paint the scene I'm sure he would have entitled it "The Failure". I was delighted when our mechanical bird burst into life once more and, after a few more bumps, sped us away from the dreary military scene.

It was not long before my spirits were restored, due mainly to J.P. who conjured up a bar of chocolate, which he shared with me, and topped it off by pouring me a cup of milky coffee from his blue flask. Such moments are priceless and J.P. was always guaranteed to provide them. Slim and good-looking as he is, he loves eating — "chomping", as he calls it — and he has an uncanny knack of finding goodies in the most unlikely places, usually in the lining of his jacket or trousers. It seems most unfair that I should struggle to control my weight, while he stays slim and lovely no matter how much he consumes!

He is considered by the learned and discerning to be one of the finest directors of documentaries in the world today. To me, he is a good friend. This friendship was cemented, or rather liquefied at 21,500 feet on Mount Everest. Whilst sharing a tent, one night, his pee bottle inadvertently decided to unscrew itself, showering us with its fulsome contents. It proved, at that height and in those conditions, to be a night to savour and remember, though it would be fair to say I infinitely preferred savouring his coffee at 2,000 feet on the Vyadoot Airways aircraft!

It intrigued me that despite the noise of the engines, I could still lose myself in the haunting qualities of the Indian landscape. It is often said that India is not a country but a continent. From north to south and east to west, the people vary greatly and the customs and language are different.

Our filming had taken us to Calcutta, a city bursting at the seams with the energy of millions of souls. I shall never forget the sight of broken-down ramshackle buses, packed to the rafters with human occupants, some holding on to the back with their fingernails as the bus rounded a corner throwing their bodies out horizontally like demented Keystone Cops.

From Calcutta we had journeyed by road, rail and plane towards the heights of Darjeeling and beyond, feasting our eyes, on vast unending plains, overcrowded towns and villages, picturesque rice fields, Hindu temples and awesome mountains. It is a place that somehow gets into your blood. Love it or hate it, you can never forget India.

Now, as we landed near Pathankot and disembarked, the strange scent of burning juniper filled the air and seduced the senses with a promise of further delightful discoveries. We set off on a three-hour taxi drive to Dharamsala. It would be fair to say that we were all thrilled to bits at the prospect of meeting the Dalai Lama. My mood put me in mind of my hero Mallory, who once said of Mount Everest: "Lord, when I think of it, something bubbles up inside me. The effervescence is sternly repressed of course . . . then a bubble outs and bursts!"

Patience! Patience! I told myself. After all, it would be two days before we could actually meet His Holiness. Also, we had a lot of filming to complete in Dharamsala before that.

The car journey was sublime. The chubby black-eyed Indian driver was warm and friendly and smiled constantly. As the journey progressed we all became quiet and still. Following the long winding road we finally reached Dharamsala itself, a village situated on various levels and cosily tucked into the hillside, with the beginnings of the giant southern Himalayas towering in the background. Such beauty! Such majesty! It was a perfect place for the Dalai Lama, the spirit of Tibet incarnate, to live.

It was now early evening and the fading sun's rays flickered like the dying embers of a fire on the dark mountains. We motored slowly through the crowded main street, our senses enraptured by the delicious aromas from small restaurants and the music which throbbed with the sound of the East. The whole place was a hive of activity and yet it was strangely harmonious. Turning into a side street, we ascended a little further and arrived at the Tibet Hotel, which proved to be a simple, plain residence, warm and comfortable. In the now surrounding darkness, it was gracefully lit by subtle pink lamps that were gentle on the eye.

My room was in the basement of the building with a single bed and three windows that looked out on a tiny courtyard. A small Tibetan lady dressed in a dark blouse and skirt, moved thither and yon around the room, as if she were on skates, demonstrating how everything worked. Once this ritual was completed, she smiled broadly, tossed me a nod and disappeared silently like a genie through the doorway. I threw myself on the bed, switched off the bedside lamp and closed my eyes. I slept deeply for an hour or so. When I awoke, I showered and joined everyone else upstairs on the veranda for refreshments.

We were all so quiet. The soft lights of Dharamsala were earthbound and did no damage to the dark of the sky and the stillness of the night. Orion and its outriders shone with a keen intensity, and the Milky Way filled the heavens with its fairy lights. In our cities, the magic of the night is invariably destroyed by our street lighting, a necessary evil, I am aware.

We sat back in our wicker chairs with legs outstretched and hummed and sighed with awe and pleasure at the splendour of it all. Later we went out to find somewhere to eat, but for the whole of that evening, we remained in this calm mood, entranced by the occupants and atmosphere of the Holy village. After a contented dinner, we returned to the hotel, whispered "good nights" and "sleep tights" and retired to our rooms. There we all slept like stones, and rose like loaves to greet one another the following morning for breakfast on the veranda.

Delicious scrambled eggs and dainty pieces of toast were placed in front of me and, rejoicing at the prospect of eating it, I allowed myself the luxury of pontificating about the meaning of life. But I paid the price for taking my eyes off my food. In the flicker of an eye, my toast was snaffled up by a big, red, hairy intruder.

"You monkey," I roared out, which was an apt description, for it was indeed such a creature, yet so fast and skilful was his action that he could easily have been mistaken for Hanuman, the Hindu monkey god himself.

With consummate ease he mounted a wall, gobbled away greedily and when he'd finished, scornfully hurled abuse at me. At the same time he eyed the kitchen door, in eager anticipation of more.

"You'll have to keep an eye on your toast here, otherwise you'll starve."

The voice belonged to a big jovial Indian gentleman,

sporting a large black moustache, who introduced himself, surprisingly, as Wally, our soundman. Then, lo and behold, behind him, much to everyone's delight, appeared our friend and Indian fixer, Shenni Italia.

Another addition to this cheerful gathering was a charming young blonde lady called Sylvia Van Kleef We owed a debt of gratitude to Sylvia, as it was through her painstaking efforts that His Holiness had agreed to be filmed. This good lady was a first-class producer in her own right, but on this occasion joined our team as Assistant Producer to J.P. It was also evident that she was totally devoted to the Dalai Lama and the Tibetan cause.

After a short discussion, tripods, cameras, and microphones were checked and, with light hearts and beaming smiles, we left the hotel and joined the souls in "Little Lhasa". With his prismatic eyes flashing excitedly, David speedily set up shots with the equally fast Veronique by his side. J.P., almost boss-eyed with the effort of keeping his fat cigar alive, flicked ash from its end to signal "Action!", and the camera rolled.

Having filmed with J.P. for a year, I was now familiar with his unique style. It is customary and universal, when making a film, for the director to give the command for action vocally. J.P., however, had a whole repertoire of silent signals. These ranged from twitching or blowing his nose, to scratching his belly or ears, breaking wind and blowing smoke rings. All were very commendable and great fun, though they could prove tricky if you were swimming a turbulent river or riding a bloody-minded Yak.

The filming in Dharamsala was no exception. Surrounded by masses of people, I giggled uncertainly until I spotted Geronimo-type smoke rings from J.P.'s Burma cheroot and galvanised myself into "action". He also rarely said "Cut" at the end of any shot. I had the feeling that he felt the effort of saying it interfered with his smoking.

During one sequence, I was under the impression that he was still filming when he wasn't, and I ended up half a mile away, disappearing into the sunset like the Sundance Kid! When I had made my way back to the film crew, I found them relaxing outside a café, eating and drinking and discussing the attributes of the airline company Cathay Pacific. On seeing me, J.P. said nonchalantly, "Oh! There you are Big Yeti!" (That's my nickname, by the way.) "We'd given you up for lost! Have a coffee! It's chomping time! Open your mouth like a good Yeti!"

I obeyed, falling on my knees to receive a delicious piece of milk chocolate. Consuming it with relish, I rose to my feet, reared backwards slightly and emitted the satisfied moans of the Big Yeti. "Ah, this is the life," I purred, sitting down and blowing on my hot coffee. "It beats working any day."

Filming continued in this fashion until half-way through the afternoon. J.P. knew exactly what he wanted, a shot here, a shot there, all simple and relaxed. Smiling contentedly at us all, he shielded his eyes from the sun and looked down for a few seconds before announcing that the filming was completed and the rest of the day was our own. We sang out a few cheerios, arranged to meet in the evening and went our separate ways.

Happy as a sand boy, I strolled down the main street and let the rhythm of the village life dictate my pace. There were nuns and monks everywhere, their bald heads and shining faces glowing with unmistakable contentment. Down the road and into the side alleys they pounded, their feet clad in well-worn rustic sandals. Dressed in dark red and faded purple robes, some proceeded in single lines alongside prayer walls (*Mani* walls) and small Buddhist temples, which contained dozens of rotating multi-coloured drums, called prayer wheels. Each devotee by turn spun these energetically until the pretty patterns shone, incandescent with the pink glow of the afternoon sun. As each drum twirled, joyously vibrating prayers into the air, the monks and nuns added their voices to the celebration by chanting, *"Om Mani Padme Hum"* — Hail the Jewel in the Lotus.

Throughout all this divine activity, the butcher, the baker, the candlestick maker and all the rest of the tradesmen of Dharamsala continued about their business. Worship and prayer seemed a natural part of everyday life, not something to focus on just one day each week. Certainly there are ritual ceremonies, such as the peaceful fire offering (*sbyin-Sregs*), but generally speaking there is no division between prayer and everyday life. It is commonplace in the stores to see people cooking and chanting at the same time.

On the street corners, old wrinkled men grinned happily at me whilst merrily spinning their hand-held prayer wheels. The hum of the village was punctuated by the sound of bicycle bells; bicycles of all shapes and sizes filled the streets, their fit riders seeking any opportunity to ring their bells and add to the music of the village.

Most fascinating of all were the workshops where numerous beautiful *thankas* were created. I suppose the simplest way to describe a *thanka* is that it is a painting on canvas, with a wooden rod through a seam at the top and the bottom — rather like a scroll. When travelling you can roll it up for convenience. *Thankas* come in all sizes and cover a multitude of stories, often relating to the Tibetan wheel of life, as well as depicting any number of demons, gods and the cycle of reincarnation.

Confounded by it all, I sat down in one of the shops and sought the expert advice of an inscrutable salesman as to which *thanka* I should buy. My new acquaintance was a small, middle-aged Tibetan who spoke English fairly fluently. During our chat, he would periodically break into a smile and casually spin his prayer wheel. Eventually he produced a fine, brightly coloured *thanka* which delighted my senses and I readily agreed to buy it. He was just about to wrap it, when I mentioned that it was my intention to give it as a gift to the Dalai Lama the following morning. The salesman drew in a deep breath and placed the *thanka* in a drawer. After careful deliberation he produced another and with deep emotion said. "Give His Holiness this one. It represents long life."

His delicate fingers lovingly packed it and covered it with a white scarf, instructing me to present the scarf first to the Dalai Lama. As I thanked him and reached the doorway he said quietly, "We wish him to live a long life."

After leaving the shop I could contain my curiosity no more. I so wanted to see where His Holiness lived. I asked passersby for directions and found everyone eager to point the way. Descending the main street for half a mile, I reached a large gate, which opened onto a steep winding path that led to the cottage where he lived, though I was unable to see it because of the dense undergrowth.

Alongside the gate was a small building that housed several officials. All was serene and peaceful. It was in complete contrast to the activity that was taking place across the street. Opposite the cottage was the Monastery of the Thekchen Choling. In its courtyard, over a hundred monks were performing a series of strange acrobatics. They took the form of balancing precariously on one leg, until the monks were in danger of falling over. At this moment they brought the other leg down vigorously, which seemed to create a kind of tense energy through their bodies. Their arms, which had been spread wide apart, came together with a loud clap. Other monks answered this clap with a clap of their own and then, after speaking for a while, would repeat the same action. It made me think of the *Commedia Dell'Arte* and of Gillian Lynne's choreography for Lowry's *Matchstick Men*.

Although so many bodies were moving at the same time, there seemed little likelihood of any collision. Intense energy, both physical and emotional, abounded, but there was no sense of frenzy. I was obviously watching some old traditional ceremony.

On crossing the road to take a closer look, I found myself the centre of attention. In my haste to explore Dharamsala, I had failed to remove my costume after filming. Consequently, I was dressed in a Norfolk Tweed jacket and Plus Fours with Puttees, not to mention a Pith helmet, which I held in my hand — all the trappings of the early 1920s. Leaning on my umbrella, I must have looked the perfect picture of the British Raj.

A motley crew of Tibetans surrounded me, and seemed to find my appearance hilarious. I gather that laughter is universal in Tibet. They certainly killed themselves laughing at me, but it was laughter of pleasure and wonder, happy polite laughter that contained no derision.

It was evident that peace and contemplation was not at all solemn to these people. Although I was aware that even the remotest understanding of Buddhism was way beyond me, I was nevertheless thoroughly enjoying its taste.

A sweet nun, speaking in broken English, explained that the monks in the courtyard were actually debating such works as *Tsong-Kha-Pa's — Essence of Eloquent Explanation*. You could, I suppose, loosely compare it with similar debates in schools, colleges and universities all over Britain. It is, of course, doubtful whether the act of clapping and playing statues would appeal to the rugby or rowing fraternity of Oxford and Cambridge. Still, the House of Commons might consider it!

After I returned to Britain, a friend of mine, Richard

Ravensdale, who works with Trek-Aid, which helps Tibetan refugees in India and Nepal, explained to me what the monks' action signified. In debate, they make a sharp pointed gesture, symbolising an arrow which is related to Manjnshri, the Buddha of Wisdom. Manjnshri holds a sword to cut through ignorance, the monks, therefore, when they wish to speak, clap their hands for attention and, after the previous monk has finished speaking and enacting the *eros* routine, receive from his outstretched hand (symbolic of both sword and arrow) his acquired knowledge.

Now, my patient reader, to return to the courtyard of the Monastery of Thekchen Choling. On closer inspection I discovered that the monks' robes were made of cotton or wool. Some wore jerkins of red and yellow. In the past, in Tibet, many monks had worn silk brocade jerkins (*stod-gag*) and brocaded shoes. In exile, following His Holiness's advice in the mid-Sixties, the robes have been standardised, but shoes are a matter of personal choice. All this information I gleaned from my enthusiastic bald friends, their glistening heads taking on a ruddy look now, for the sun was low in the sky and its almost horizontal rays turned the green trees a dazzling vermilion. Everything seemed almost surreal.

The Monastery itself perfectly encapsulated the wonder of the place. Work was started on this building in 1970. Quarters were also built for the monks. Inauguration day was attended by His Holiness in 1974. In 1976, for the first time outside Tibet, nine new students were taught sacred dance and they performed the Black Hat Dance for the first time in

India. On this momentous day, His Holiness gave a certain commentary to the Kalachakra Sadhana, to the Abbot, Ritual Master and other monks, and yellow-hatted monks supporting the long horns blew out a joyful message to the world that 20,000 Tibetan people were alive and well and living in Dharamsala.

The sun was now sinking rapidly and I tried to say goodbye because I was determined to see the sun set high above the village. But several jolly monks would have none of it. Taking me by the arm, they insisted on showing me the Children's Village.

After a short journey, we arrived outside the settlement where the children lived. I could hear happy, young animated voices reverberating everywhere but I refrained from entering, as I judged that my appearance would cause an uproar. My suspicion was justified. Several children running down a dirt road towards the gate caught a glimpse of me and collapsed in paroxysms of mirth. Unable to contain themselves, they rushed into a nearby house to tell their friends of their discovery, which resulted in yet more laughter. Then scores of them crammed every window to get a good look at me and positively howled with raucous delight.

During this mayhem, I beat a hasty retreat to a nearby clump of trees and made myself as invisible as possible. There, the monks imparted the story of the children.

The Tibetan Children's Village in Dharamsala has about 750 children, who come from the seven major Tibetan settlements in central and southern India. These children are mainly orphaned or from the very poor among the Tibetan settlers. In the village they are given a home and education. It was important, the monks maintained, for the children to grow up in a truly Tibetan atmosphere, so that they could keep alive their national language and customs; having been born in India, they have never seen or known their own country first-hand.

After popping my head round a tree to ascertain that the coast was clear, I strolled back, with my amused friends in attendance, towards the Tibet Hotel. The monks explained to me that the schools for children were part of a larger organisation, which was attempting to give work and identity to all exiled Tibetans. As we moved into the side streets, it was clear for all to see that they were succeeding.

In their flight over the mountains from Chinese aggression in 1959, the Tibetans realised that the one thing they had brought with them was the traditional culture of Tibet, and that this could be their salvation. Business was one of these Tibetan skills learnt from trading with surrounding countries, and it was to prove of vital importance. As I arrived outside my hotel, I bowed respectfully, thanked my kind guides and shook their hands, hoping to see them on the morrow. Then I proceeded up the hill towards the mountains.

I moved quickly, gaining height rapidly and, after half an hour, reached the outskirts of the village. Great mountains loomed ahead of me. I estimated them at about 17,000 feet. If only I had wings and could fly over them, I thought. Then I would be able to see the Great Indus and Brahmaputra rivers rise together to flow in opposite directions down the gorges by which they break through to the Himalayas in one direction and the Indian Ocean in the other.

A mile further on I came to a river, which streamed from the base of the mountains. Here I stopped and took in the scenery. My escape had taken me past buildings of white and green, some half finished, with workers singing gaily. Many of these buildings were half-covered by clematis orientalis which grows prolifically everywhere, clambering over walls and trees and blooming in a staggering range of colours, from apricot-yellow to almost black. Sadly, by contrast, the rhododendron season was over. Particularly sad for me, as I live surrounded by that shrub back home, and would dearly have loved to have seen those of Little Lhasa. The life on and around the river would have delighted the character Ratty in *Toad of Toad Hall*. There were Ruddy Shelducks, Indian Brahminy ducks and Bar Headed geese. What looked like Sand Martins cut through the air, and Giant Lammingers soared overhead. How odd that such a bird should emit such a tiny mouse-like cry! Red Billed Choughs and Pied Wagtails were among the throng and many varied doves.

I sometimes feel that the magpie must be the most successful bird in the world; needless to say, they populate every nook and cranny around Dharamsala. But the birds did not have it all their own way. They had to contest their space with exuberant kite-flying enthusiasts. Kites of all shapes and colours tossed and soared and flickered down like pretty lunar moths. Kite-flying is a traditional hobby with the Tibetans. They have been flying kites for over 2,000 years.

Kites, birds, and white prayer flags danced bewitchingly to the music that filled the air. Hundreds of pure white prayer flags fluttered like clouds of cabbage white butterflies. Prayers in praise of Buddha vibrated from these flags; cascading down the hill sides, they sent their tremulous offerings throughout the world, for the good of mankind.

The darkening azure blue sky heralded the demise of the day. The gentle breeze that had assisted the kites had now gone to rest. All was still.

Quietly, I rose and gazed at the last shimmering flames of our mother star's fiery splendour. In that moment I murmured the words of Wordsworth's "Tintern Abbey":

> And I have felt
> A presence that disturbs me with the joy
> Of elevated thoughts; a sense sublime
> Of something far more deeply interfused,
> Whose dwelling is the light of setting suns,
> And the round ocean and the living air,
> And the blue sky, and in the mind of man:
> A motion and a spirit, that impels
> All thinking things, all objects of all thought,
> And rolls through all things.

Back at the Tibet Hotel, reclining in an easy chair on the veranda with the lacy tapestry of the Milky Way kissing my face and the rhythm of my breathing seemingly almost at a standstill, I effortlessly meditated and felt myself at one with the warm cloak of night. Later I was joined by the rest of the film crew. We were aware that we had all shared similar experiences. The day had been out of this world for everyone, the only discordant note being poor Sylvia who had a wretched cold, though this did not in any way affect her cheerful disposition. The gallant lass, after eating some fruit and taking her medicine, excused herself and retired to bed. Lit by the gentle lamps of the veranda, the rest of us enjoyed a light meal that was made up of rice, noodles and a plentiful salad.

It is curious that after experiencing such a deep meditation I should then proceed to be rather loud and bawdy, instead of sensitive and spiritual. The mood was wholeheartedly shared by everyone, and we laughed fit to bust, atavistic laughter like the laughter we had shared on Everest at 22,000 feet. David, his prismatic eyes weeping with so much mirth, said through bouts that he had never met anyone to even compare to me for out and out bullshit! Everyone nodded in full agreement. David is always floored by my ability to add on noughts — 10,000 becomes 100,000 and so on. My bank manager, my agent, my P.A. and my wife have learnt over the years how to sift and refine my excesses. I have simply always preferred magic to facts. David calls it "hedgehogging".

"How many hedgehogs high is Everest, Brian?"

He knows all there is to know about climbing and mountains and I over-decorate my replies in order to see David and J.P. double up with mirth. And so, on that blissful evening, I "hedgehogged" away to their great delight. Then David and Veronique fervently begged me to imitate the American actor George C. Scott, as General Patton in the film *Lust for Glory*. For the next twenty minutes I did so, culminating with Patton's words when his army defeats Rommel's in the desert. "You magnificent bastard! I read yer book."

On all our minds, you see, was the priceless prospect of meeting His Holiness in the morning. It was this anticipation that inspired the closeness and camaraderie of that special evening. After much hugging we said goodnight.

J.P., like the kind soul that he is, had arranged for me to be moved upstairs just off the veranda, as my room in the basement had proved a little damp. After a quick shower I switched off the light and was just about to get into bed when, through my window, in the house on the other side of the street, I observed a venerable old man performing a ceremony. Backwards and forwards he rocked, all the while chanting various mantras in a soft voice. I became absorbed in his total devotion. The walls in his room were covered with *thankas*, and prayer lamps burnt with a gentle zeal. The scene had a friendly haunting quality. He read aloud from different texts, pausing now and then to ring a little hand bell. Every action was so gentle. On he went until I was convinced that he had reached the climax of the ceremony — only for him to start all over again with a different mantra and further rocking.

As he wrapped a white scarf around his neck and placed his hands together in supplication, I moved away from the window and lay down on my bed. From this position I could still see the old boy and his distant chanting was soothing to the senses. What did it all mean?

The whole of Dharamsala throbbed with chanting. You couldn't help being influenced by it. The very air sang with the sounds of Buddhism. Yet, as much as I had let myself merge into the spirit of it all, I was still a Briton with centuries of Celtic, Roman, Saxon, Viking and Norman influence.

In the morning I would meet the Dalai Lama and I was uneasy about it. Prior to coming on this adventure, scores of people had expressed to me their deep desire to meet him. With genuine emotion they moaned and sighed and wrung their hands together with frustrated longing to see His Holiness. Why? I asked myself, as I lay on my bed. Why do people want to meet him? Why does he have this effect? Who is he? What is he?

My mind raced. Was it because in this mechanised world of fax machines, computers and instant results, we have eliminated personal growth and fulfilment? Have we created a technology that dominates our thinking? Do video games and the like annihilate our capacity for creative dreaming? Does the Dalai Lama, therefore, represent something that we have lost? That may be it, I thought, as I looked at the ceiling of my room. Lost! We have lost something. Certainly, when some people think of His Holiness, they see a smiling kind face, a face that comes from a remote strange land. Maybe in their hearts they yearn for peace and happiness, for a hidden place like Shangri La in the novel *Lost Horizon*. A mysterious faraway place, where hearts are joined in an atmosphere of unlimited growth and bliss. Maybe this is what His Holiness, this holder of the Nobel Peace Prize, means to people.

When I thought about it, the prospect of my meeting this smiling gentleman perplexed me. It was ridiculous! What was I really doing here? I was Brian Blessed, a Yorkshire lad, son of a coal miner, who had become an actor and been on a few adventures. To be sure, I was here to repeat a ceremony that had taken place in 1920, covering Sir Charles Bell's visit, but somehow I felt a fake. The Dalai Lama had better things to do than make a film! His nation and the whole world needed his help. Every second of his time was precious. In the final analysis, it didn't make sense.

Pausing a while to pour myself a cold drink, I gazed through the window at the old man. He was still completely absorbed in prayer. A combination of Attila the Hun's army and the audience at *The Last Night of the Proms* would not have disturbed him. Oh! The power of Buddhism! Amazing!

My mind was still fermenting. Who is the Dalai Lama? Just a fella, or a God? They say he is a God-King. But people aren't gods, are they? Wizards don't exist, do they? Do the small Chorten buildings all over the Buddhist lands really hold down demons? Is it really possible for people to fly? Apparently, in the past, several holy men have projected themselves through the air. In the eighth century, Guru Bimpoche, the second Buddha, mounted a flying tiger and landed at a point in Bhutan, later named Taktsang, which means "Tiger's Den", and brought Buddhism to that country.

Yes indeed! It's a very holy place. Pilgrims come from all over Bhutan to worship there. But surely only Sabu, in the film *The Thief of Bagdad* can fly on a magic carpet. Surely it is only sensible to dismiss any notion that the Dalai Lama could conceivably be a God-King! After all, His Holiness often says of himself, "I'm just a simple Buddhist monk — no more, no less." There, you see, right from the horse's mouth. So what is all the fuss about? After all, I thought, I often help the Tibetan cause. The history of the country has always fascinated me.

Out of interest, the name Dalai Lama used not to be used in Tibet at all. The great Mongolian ruler Altan Khan, who had embraced Buddhism, gave the title "Dalai Lama" to the incarnations. Dalai Lama means, literally, "broad ocean".

Rather than risk confusing the issue, let me give you a few facts about the Holy man.

His Holiness, the fourteenth Dalai Lama, Tenzin Gyatso, is the head of state and spiritual leader of the Tibetan people. He was born Lhamo Dhondrub, on 6 July 1935, in a small village called Taktser in northern Tibet. Born to a peasant family, His Holiness was recognised at the age of two, in accordance with Tibetan tradition, as the reincarnation of his predecessor, the thirteenth Dalai Lama, and thus an incarnation of Avalokitesvara, the Buddha of Compassion.

The Dalai Lamas are the manifestations of the Bodhisattva (Buddha) of Compassion, who chose to reincarnate to serve the people. Lhamo Dhondrub was, as Dalai Lama, renamed Jetsun Jamphel Ngawang

Lobsang Yeshe Tenzin Gyatso — "Holy Lord, Gentle Glory, Compassionate, Defender of the Faith, Ocean of Wisdom". Tibetans normally refer to His Holiness as Yeshe Norbu, "The Wish Fulfilling Gem", or simply Kundun, "The Presence".

The enthronement ceremony took place on 22 February 1940 in Lhasa, the capital of Tibet. At this time His Holiness received new names such as "The Tender, Glorious One", "The Mighty of Speech", "The Excellent Understanding". Although he was only five years old, everyone was astonished at the dignity of the child and the gravity with which he followed ceremonies which lasted for hours.

I am informed that the education of a Dalai Lama is mind-blowingly difficult. His Holiness began his education at the age of six and completed the Geshe Lharampa degree (Doctorate of Buddhist Philosophy) when he was twenty-five in 1959. He then took the preliminary examinations at each of the three monastic universities: Drepung, Sera and Ganden. The final examination was conducted in the Jokhang, Lhasa, during the annual Monlam Festival of Prayer, held in the first month of every year in the Tibetan calendar.

Today he often states with wry humour that he is undoubtedly the most unfortunate Dalai Lama in history. In the same breath he maintains that he is also probably the most fortunate, being in a positive position to help his people. He has displayed tremendous courage all his life. Imagine the heavy responsibility placed on his shoulders on 17 November 1950, when he was only fifteen years old. He was then called upon to assume full political power as Head of State and Government, after a massive modern Chinese army invaded Tibet, attacking its frontiers in six places simultaneously. The ill-equipped Tibetan army could not possibly defend itself against such a mighty force. The Tibetan soldiers were gallant in the defence of their country, but the outcome was a forgone conclusion and the Tibetan army was routed.

In 1954, His Holiness went to Beijing to talk peace with Mao Tse-Tung and other Chinese leaders, including Chou En-Lai and Deng Xiaoping. In 1956, while visiting India to attend the 2500th Buddha Jayanti Anniversary, he had a series of meetings with Prime Minister Nehru and Premier Chou about deteriorating conditions in Tibet.

His efforts to bring about a peaceful solution to the Sino-Tibetan conflict were thwarted by the ruthless Beijing policy in eastern Tibet, which ignited a popular uprising and resistance. This resistance movement spread to other parts of the country.

On 10 March 1959, the capital of Tibet, Lhasa, exploded with the largest demonstration calling on China to leave Tibet and reaffirming Tibet's independence. All was chaos within the capital and everyone was fearful for the safety of the Dalai Lama, as he had been invited by a Chinese General to a stage show inside the Chinese army camp. Several thousand Tibetans formed a human shield around the Dalai Lama's summer palace, declaring that they would stop him from accepting the invitation. As the tension mounted, it was the magnificent Tibetan Khampas who miraculously assisted His Holiness to make his astonishing flight to India. But appalling battles followed. Thousands of Tibetans perished before the rebellion was finally crushed by Chinese tanks and artillery.

Some 80,000 Tibetan refugees followed His Holiness into India. Today there are more than 120,000 Tibetans in exile, and His Holiness has resided in Dharamsala since 1960.

Well, my gallant readers, it's a lot to take in, eh? What devastating days they must have been. Out of the darkness of the holocaust, the Dalai Lama and his followers constituted a new Tibetan government-in-exile. He realised that his immediate and most urgent task was to save the Tibetan exiles and their culture. The Tibetan Institute for Performing Arts was established in 1959, while the Central Institute of Higher Tibetan Studies became a university for Tibetans in India. Over 200 monasteries have been re-established to preserve the vast corpus of Tibetan Buddhist teachings. This influence stretches even as far as Scotland. Strange to think that that beautiful country has a harbour that contains giant black nuclear "Moby Dick" submarines, while in the Firth of Clyde, one mile off the coast of Arran, is the Holy Island project, which has recently celebrated the inauguration of the new Samye Temple at the Kagyu Samye Ling Tibetan Centre.

Aye, they say God works in mysterious ways. Yet, as I lay back on my pillow with all these facts buzzing through my brain, I still could not visualise myself speaking to His Holiness. How did I "fit in"? Amusingly, give or take a few months we were the same age. Other comparisons were ludicrous.

When I was a young working-class lad in South Yorkshire, going out with my dad to swim in the local canal in 1944, His Holiness was busying himself in a very different manner. He was behind the glass front of a sedan chair, carried by dedicated powerful bearers. Behind him came grooms leading his favourite horses, all splendidly caparisoned. Their bridles were yellow and their bits and saddles glistened with pure gold. Four Cabinet ministers rode on splendid horses on either side of the sovereign. Then came a flock of high dignitaries and senior members of the God-King's household, the latter all monks with the rank of Abbot. Alongside them marched the tall figures of the bodyguards — huge fellows over six foot six inches tall, chosen for their size and strength. Then followed the commander-in-chief of the army. He held his sword at the salute. Behind, came another magnificent chair, carried by more bearers, in which sat the Regent, Tagtra Gyeltsap Bimpoche, styled "The Tiger Rock". After him rode the representatives of the Tree of Pillars of the State, the Abbots of Sera, Drebung and Ganden. Then approached the yellow, silk-lined palanquin of the living Buddha, gleaming like gold in the sunlight. The bearers were six-and-thirty men in green silk coats, wearing red hats. A monk was holding a huge iridescent sun-shade made of peacock feathers over the palanquin.

Gradually, the procession vanished behind the gates of the summer palace. That must have been a happy day for the God-King, escaping the lonely life in the gigantic, somewhat gloomy Potala Palace for his summer residence in Norbulinga, with its lovely peach trees and delightful gardens.

I'm sure if I could have visited him in those days, he would have loved playing with my Dinky toys and reading about World Heavyweight Boxing Champion — Joe Louis in my scrapbook. After all, I know for a fact that boxing has always interested him. Yes! I thought, as I looked up at the ceiling of my hotel room, I'm sure His Holiness and I will have much in common when we meet tomorrow!

Imitating the action of the monks in the courtyard of the Thekchen Choling Monastery, I balanced on one leg, then brought the other down vigorously and shot my arms out, sending my imaginary arrow straight through the bedroom window to the still chanting old man. Let him sort out my befuddled mind, I thought. With that I climbed back into bed and slept like a baby.

The next morning at 10 a.m. sharp, we were outside the gate leading to the Dalai Lama's home, having our passport and papers inspected by meticulous officials. The sun was up and the sky was clear.

Without further ado we were allowed to proceed. Thrilled to bits, I walked speedily ahead of the rest of the crew, as they paused to check out their equipment. The rather steep winding path really did make me feel as though I was following the Yellow Brick Road. On either side were lawns and bushes covered in flowers. But I'm afraid I was not paying much attention to detail. When I arrived at His Holiness's cottage, I was in such an excitable state of mind that to this day I cannot remember exactly what the building looked like. (Strange, because I have always had a photographic memory.) As far as I can recall, it was rather like a cheerful villa. What really caught my attention was a large gathering of monks outside the front door. They were colourfully dressed in red and yellow robes, and their hats were simply amazing — similar, in style to those worn by the Spartan warriors in ancient Greece, but vibrant yellow in colour.

I felt shy, retreated, and sat on the lawn opposite. They were preparing for a huge festival that would take place at the Thekchen Choling Monastery the following day. They seemed more excited than I was and, after much clasping and nods, they went their merry way.

All was quiet until J.P. and the crew joined me. Together we were allowed to enter the cottage, where a smiling young monk introduced us to the Dalai Lama's interpreter. He was a charming Tibetan gentleman of medium stature, dressed in a long black shirt and dark trousers. He kindly explained that His Holiness spoke good English but that he was there to smooth over any hiccups. I think the interpreter found my Twenties' outfit somewhat disconcerting, and it was noticeable that he periodically gripped his face so as not to laugh. It was obvious that his diplomacy was being tested to the full!

We were led into a large cheerful room with light-brown wooden French windows opening out onto the garden. The walls were powder blue, which contrasted perfectly with the natural colour of the big windows. The curtains were subtle with beige flowers and the floor was covered with wall-to-wall green carpet, which had red patterned Tibetan rugs liberally scattered upon it. There were many ancient chests most beautifully decorated and the walls were adorned with splendid *thankas* illustrating the Lama's previous lives. These were in both the old *men-sar* and the new *men-ri* styles, and were rich with colour, red and gold dazzling the eyes.

Two light-green armchairs had been provided for the interview and they had been half covered in white sheets. While the crew busied themselves setting up the camera and lights (lights are always tricky when filming), I moved over to the French windows, which were open, and walked out into the garden. Several young monks had gathered there and my closeness caused them to smile and giggle.

Then, out of nowhere, appeared a middle-aged monk of medium height, dressed in red with a dash of yellow and wearing slightly tinted glasses with light-red frames. He radiated health and happiness. It was none other than the Dalai Lama.

He placed his beaming face close to mine, chuckling all the while, and enquired in a warm deep voice, "Is it time to start filming?"

"Not quite yet, Your Holiness," I replied. "In about another ten minutes."

"Oh! Good, good, good," he answered, laughing quietly to himself. Then with a twinkle in his eye he continued, "You are the Blessed man, who go to Everest, yes?"

"Yes," I responded. "My name is Brian Blessed,

though I am not much blessed. I come to you for that. And you I know are the Dalai Lama."

His Holiness nodded and chuckled away again, saying, "So they tell me."

We both then became quiet and he scrutinised me closely, though never for a moment losing the twinkle in his eye. Then his face formed a tiny smile, which grew and grew and grew until his cheek bones protruded and glistened with fun.

I was deeply moved and he held both my hands. This made me frightfully shy and prompted me to say bluntly, "It is so strange meeting a God-King. You are a God-King, aren't you?"

The statement took his breath away and he bent over double with laughter. It was a high-pitched laugh, in contrast to his deep voice. Holding his stomach he managed, "No, no, no, not God-King, just a simple monk."

To which I replied, "Well, Your Holiness, if you are a simple monk, then I'm a Dutchman."

This made him laugh even more and prompted J.P., who with David and Veronique was still struggling with the lighting, to shout to me in the garden, "I hope you're behaving yourself with His Holiness."

"Oh yes," I shouted back. "We're getting on famously."

This convivial atmosphere seemed to bewilder the gentle interpreter somewhat and he voiced his reservations by saying, "It is difficult! His Holiness does not normally receive such questions."

His Holiness was now most eager to get on with it but

David was still not satisfied with the lighting. He was a perfectionist and that was that. Therefore, I continued to hold the fort. With the diplomacy of a woolly Yeti, I endeavoured to charm and restrain His Holiness.

"You used to like boxing when you lived in Lhasa," I said.

"Oh yes," he replied. "Much — how you say — boxing in Lhasa, and horse riding, wrestling and games. I was not very good at boxing."

As he finished saying this, he affected a mock pugilistic stance, which I matched. The interpreter was getting more agitated by the minute. Undaunted, I pressed on with more questions.

"Do you know if the elephant that the Maharaja of Nepal gave you when you were a boy in Tibet is still alive?"

This question surprised him and he gazed at me in amazement.

"I think when I leave Tibet, it was well, in very, very big stables. No one in Tibet ever see such a big animal!"

"Yes," I added, "he was such a gigantic animal, they called him *Langchen Rimpoche* (Large Abbot). After travelling the 700-mile route to Lhasa, the elephant was given a house of his own on the north side of Potala."

"Yes," replied the Dalai Lama, incredulously. "That is true! Oh, it seems only — how you say — yesterday."

The end of the discussion about the elephant coincided perfectly with the all-clear for filming to commence and we made ourselves comfortable on the white- sheeted armchairs. J.P. scratched his nose, which meant "Action", and I started the ball rolling.

"Well, Your Holiness, it's a great privilege to be here. It's so peaceful! I must look so ridiculous to you with my pith helmet and umbrella. These are the clothes I wore on Everest."

At this point I showed him my period boots in greater detail. His Holiness was having great difficulty keeping his face straight. There is no doubt that he found me a complete hoot. It was great fun and I was relaxing and enjoying myself.

"Of course," he continued, "it is your will power, your will, to go to Everest in such clothes."

His Holiness was completely at ease on camera and his English was quite impressive. If the roles had been reversed I would have had hell speaking in Tibetan. We British are so vain, we expect everyone to speak our language.

We completed the first part of the filming by enacting the ceremony that had been performed by the thirteenth Dalai Lama and Sir Charles Bell in 1920. We then proceeded to discuss the mighty mountain itself. The mood changed and the Dalai Lama eased himself forward in the chair.

"Yes," he said quietly, "Chomolungma (Everest) is considered a very sacred mountain, the one where we believe the famous deities, the sisters, to be. Originally they came from India, then eventually moved to the main Himalayan regions. They have the responsibility of looking after Buddhist teaching in Tibet, while we are in exile. They bring Padma Samblava, the famous

Indian Buddhist saint, to the Za-Rong-Puck (Rongbuk) Monastery on Everest. So the mountain is guardian for Tibetan Buddhist teaching. Besides its height and beauty, I consider it very important. In Tibetan we call it *Yankiamuntakim* because of the height. The top of the mountain appears to touch the blue sky. The name *Yankiamun* — how do you say — means 'The Majesty, The Queen of Snow Mountain'. *Tinkin*, means blue, er dark blue. So *Yankiamuntakim* means 'The Queen of the Blue Snow Mountain in the Sky'."

As he finished these words, we joined hands in a few seconds of silence, which I broke by saying, "Yes, Your Holiness. Today many people in Tibet, the Yak herders for instance, call Everest 'The Turquoise Mountain'. It is interesting that it is so big and huge and is not a God but a Goddess."

His Holiness chuckled at this, saying, "Female most important in creation."

At this point J.P. twitched his nose, which signalled "Cut", and David announced that he was changing his camera position and there would be a short break while he adjusted the lights. This gave me the chance to pursue a few questions of my own. His Holiness was patience itself.

"I have heard that at the base of Everest, on the Tibetan side by Rongbuk, monks and nuns have experienced *Cho*, the ritual confrontation of all that frightens one; and *Tsai Lung*, the control of energy through what is known as 'The Channels of Wind', a form of breathing which relates to the pulse of the universe."

"Yes, yes, this is so," replied His Holiness.

I had his full attention now and he held my left hand tightly. Pausing to collect my thoughts, as I had listed so many things to ask him, I spied J.P. smiling from across the room, obviously delighted with my involvement with the great man. Receiving a warm nod from him I carried on with my questions.

"Your Holiness, I have heard that mystics, for hundreds of years now, have lived in remote caves in the area around Everest, Gyachung Kang and Makalu, pitting themselves against the forces of life, death and being. These places are in the Sacred Hidden Valleys of the Himalaya that you call *Be-Yul*. They are the 'Power Places' that emanate the Life Force and are the Navel of the Planet. There, the mystics spend their entire lives in meditation."

"This is true too," smiled His Holiness. "But this can also be done in your own home." He patted my cheek. "No need to go to so much trouble."

By now everyone was listening to our discussion, so I decided to be naughty and change the subject.

"Your Holiness," I enquired, "you are obviously a vegetarian. Have you never eaten meat?"

"Oh yes," he smiled. "When I was a young man I tried some dried Yak meat. It was delicious! To this day I still miss it and long for some. But no, I cannot have any. I am Dalai Lama."

I must mention that, by this stage the interpreter was holding a hand to his forehead and looking distinctly sick. Enjoying myself like a five-year-old, I plunged on.

"Tell me, Your Holiness, how do you cope with the

flies and mosquitos when they rest on your body and threaten your health?"

Grinning from ear to ear, he replied, "When mosquito land on my arm, I blow it off. If same mosquito repeat same action, I flick it away gently with my finger. If same mosquito do the same again, I slap my hand down and crush it. It is practical."

"I wish to ask you another question," I said, which received a chorus of groans from everyone present. Not so His Holiness. He smiled radiantly and said, "No, I like this, he ask me questions no one else does."

Delighted to hear this, I carried on.

"Tell me, Your Holiness, the Chinese have knocked hell out of your country and continue to commit all kinds of atrocities against your people, yet I heard somewhere that you consider the Chinese to have given you your greatest opportunity for personal development. In other words, to learn to love them. Do you love them?"

There was a long silence. The interpreter at that point was in danger of taking a running jump down the nearest ravine. His Holiness, the Wish-Fulfilling Gem, the Gentle Glory, Compassionate, Defender of the Faith, Kundun, the Presence, Ocean of Wisdom and an incarnation of Avalokitesvara, the Buddha of Compassion said, "Yes, I do love them."

Holding my hands again, he drew me closer and proceeded, saying, "How do you say in the West? It is the final acid test. Easy to love nearest and dearest, but to love enemy is not so easy. You see, Mr Blessed, I love my people and my country, also I feel sorry for Chinese in Tibet. I do not believe they are really happy there, the climate does not suit them. So when we Tibetans finally have our country back, and have our own democratic government, I see no reason why some Chinese, if they wish, should not come and live with us. All this must be achieved peacefully. It is the only way."

I bowed and thanked him and squeezed in one more question, while the interpreter appeared to be in need of smelling salts!

"Your Holiness, have you ever felt anger towards anyone?"

"Oh yes," he answered immediately. "A while ago I received a needle injection in my arm for protection when travelling. It was very painful, because the doctor caught my muscle with the point. I was in agony, running around the room, I wanted to hit him. I kept saying, 'Oh that fat doctor, I hate him, I want to hit him.' He was a big fat doctor, he was even fatter than . . ."

At this point His Holiness grabbed his mouth, for he was looking straight at me. I completed his sentence.

"I see, Your Holiness, you mean he was fatter than me! Oh, Your Holiness, I am hurt, I am cut to the quick, I shall never be the same again. To think that you, the Dalai Lama of ancient Tibet is comparing me to a fat doctor!"

The whole room was now in uproar, that is except for the interpreter who continued to chunter, "It is difficult. His Holiness is not usually asked these questions." He seemed very much in need of a fat doctor himself.

His Holiness, full of fun, bent down low in front of me and with outstretched hands pretended to beg for my forgiveness.

Immediately I responded by saying, "Oh, Your Holiness, have no fear, I forgive you for your transgression."

"Oh! Thank you, thank you, so much," whispered the great man in mock relief, and we both sat down.

Then he utterly surprised me when he massaged the base of my left thumb and said, "Not to worry about your brother. He will be all right. He live a long life."

I must explain. I had never mentioned my brother to the Dalai Lama, or that he was ill.

"Tell him, if he does not believe in God, to always think of people he loves and things he likes."

I replied, "Well, he loves his family, and his home is all and everything to him. And he likes his car. I understand that when you lived in Lhasa you had a car?"

"Oh yes, I did," he answered, sighing with remembrance. "It was a big car, yellow and black."

"Yes, Your Holiness," I went on. "I'm afraid it is all broken and rusty in an old stable-yard in the Norbalinka Summer Palace. I have seen it on film. It is a Dodge, I think, and trees now grow through its engine. It is a tourist attraction."

My words made him quiet and he nodded slowly, his eyes pensive and melancholy. We then talked about his collection of watches and clocks, some of which he inherited from the thirteenth Dalai Lama. His favourite piece was an Omega calendar clock. How funny, I thought: here was a man who appeared limitless and not concerned with the rags of time, yet he actually mended watches as a hobby. I also referred to his eye-glasses, which I thought were very attractive. He said he had worn them for years, his first pair having been given to him by the Indian Legation, when he lived at the Potala Palace.

I asked him about his horses and did he still ride? I had read that he made his famous escape from Tibet on horseback. He found this question amusing.

"I am not very interested in horses," he confessed. "It is funny that the former body (meaning the thirteenth Dalai Lama) was fond of horses and that they mean so little to me."

When the filming finally came to an end, His Holiness presented me with a beautiful patterned silk scarf, which he wished me to place on the summit of Mount Everest, in the name of peace. He also asked me to recite the mantra *Om Mani Padme Hum* (Hail Jewel in the Lotus Flower) for the good of mankind. He then added a more complex and private mantra for me to chant in homage of the Goddess Mother of Earth.

My heart brimming with emotion, I bowed and thanked the Holy Lord. Then I sat in a far corner of the room, absolutely shattered by the whole experience, and shared a bowl of fruit with the interpreter. We were just about to have a chat when he was called back into the fray, as first J.P. and then Sylvia interviewed His Holiness. Both interviews were quite political in content and way above my head. J.P. is such a clever lad.

It was now time to go, as it was lunchtime and the Dalai Lama loves his food. We would see him the following day in the village when he made his rounds, and so we would leave our farewells until then. We were courteously escorted to the door by the relieved interpreter and we made our way back down the hill.

We were all thrilled to smithereens, punching the air and congratulating each other. It had been a marvellous day. "What a team!" I thought.

Before we split up, J.P. informed me that he wished to film a blink shot with me, a shot taken just as the sun is setting. He had chosen his favourite tea-house for it, which he said overlooked a gorgeous valley. Several hours later I met him there with David, Veronique and Wally. It certainly was a stunning setting. Made of old seasoned timber, with a large open window, the tea-house overlooked a deep green meandering valley. The foothills of the Himalayas were in the distance and were already flaming in anticipation of the sunset.

"Ah, marvellous, J.P.," I murmured.

"Isn't it just," replied my friend. "And look, Brian, what I have found you! No, not a bar of chocolate, but a sweet Buddhist nun, who comes from Los Angeles."

Stepping aside, like a naughty Master of Ceremonies, he revealed a young, thin, bald, pretty nun with a cheerful face.

"Hello, Brian," she whispered mischievously. "My name is Feather, and I come from LA, though I live here and help His Holiness when he travels abroad. My given Buddhist name is Thubten Wangmo."

J.P. then said that he wished to film us together with the sunset behind us, but as the sun would not be in the correct position for at least another half-hour, he begged to be excused, as he wanted to film something else in the village. With that, he was gone, leaving me with the thin nun.

It transpired that she was a Jewish princess and a millionairess, who had given up all that side of her life to be a nun, though she retained some of her wealth to arrange transport for the Dalai Lama's emissaries when they visited the USA. Feather was quite terrific, like an open book, describing her daily life and the scores of mantras that existed in Buddhism. I told her about my day, which made her both laugh and cry. We conversed for an hour or so until the sun disappeared and the hill slept. When J.P. finally returned, it was too late to film, but we spent the evening together, eating peacefully by the glow of butterlamps (lamps that burn butter!).

That evening, in my room back at the hotel, I was far too excited to sleep. Every time I closed my eyes I saw the Dalai Lama's smiling face and heard his high-pitched laugh. My thoughts turned to an American called Jeff Long, from Boulder, Colorado, with whom I had shared a tent at 19,800 feet on the East Rongbuk glacier of Everest, a few months earlier.

Jeff was a first-rate mountaineer who had been my minder. He was a veritable giant, powerfully built and over six and a half feet tall. As giants go, he was a kind, sensitive, self-effacing one, and he was also a successful author. He was a champion of people's rights and used his pen to fight the good fight. The Tibetan cause was dear to his heart and he had been imprisoned for months in various jails in Nepal in the late Seventies. He was as brave as a lion and tender as a lamb.

We made a strange pair at that high camp, he rather

introverted, whereas I — well, need I say more? That evening, high on the mountain, he told me an amazing story about a legendary Khampa leader, a warrior called Wangdu, who lived somewhere in a hidden fortress in the pink hills of the mystical country of Mustang, traditionally known as the Land of Lo. Jeff likened Wangdu to Sitting Bull and Geronimo in American history. Remember, it was the Khampas who had miraculously saved the Dalai Lama's life at the Potala Palace. Fierce and independent, they had never surrendered to the Chinese invaders.

The almost mythical Wangdu emerged at night from his stronghold in the heart of Lo. He and his horsemen on swift, light-brown horses with blond manes, and big, black, bald-headed hunting dogs, would terrorise the Chinese invaders of Tibet. Once their objectives were accomplished, they would retire back again to the pink dry hills of Mustang, like so many ghosts. Wangdu infuriated the Chinese, as they were not permitted to enter Mustang.

Jeff told me that Wangdu's actions inspired America's Central Intelligence Agency to secretly supply weapons and funds for their guerrilla activities in the mid-Sixties. Volunteers were taken to a remote military installation in the Colorado mountains for special training. In their desperate fight for freedom, Wangdu and his fighters set up bases all over Mustang. One, at Lori Gomp, was called "Soldier Mountain".

After a considerable pause, Jeff continued: "Oh, Brian, Tibet is a tragedy. China's illegal occupation of the country is one of the great crimes against humanity in this century. They have killed over one million people in Tibet, one sixth of the population. Thousands were transported into labour camps, their children removed for indoctrination. According to the International Commission of Jurists, they have violated human rights in Tibet in no less than sixteen different ways, including murder, rape, torture and the destruction of family life. The People's Republic of China continues systematically to plunder and destroy the Tibetan culture and environment. God, Brian! They are using Tibet as a nuclear dumping ground and testing site! What was once Shangri La, however imperfect, is now a graveyard and Gulag, garrisoned by Chinese troops and overrun by seven and a half million Chinese colonists!"

Jeff's words on that great mountain that day had appalled me. Now, here I was sitting in my hotel room in Dharamsala, after a great day, still troubled. I ask you: what does it mean invading a country? I've never experienced it!

The closest I have come to smelling invasion was an occasion when I was a guest on *Breakfast Time* with Selina Scott. It was during the Miners' Strike of 1984. Suddenly the screens in the studio flashed pictures of Goldthorpe in Yorkshire, where I lived as a child and where my mother, father, brother, his wife and two children still reside today. Hundreds of police were charging down the streets with shields, scattering the citizens. I could not comprehend it. These were the people of Goldthorpe, my people, sweet kind people, hard-working and law-abiding, who had lived and died in the coal mines, who had dignity second to none and, who were the salt of the earth, and they were being "invaded". I was incensed! At that moment in the studio, I would have been glad to have Wangdu at my side and to have wrought havoc on the police!

Well, that day has passed and Goldthorpe is quiet and peaceful once more, but the scars will take a long time to heal. But what of Tibet?

It is clear that the Dalai Lama feels nothing but love and nurtures only love in his parishioners. How is this possible? What happens to rage and revenge? The Buddhists of Dharamsala warm the very centre of your heart with their love.

The following day I watched J.P. film His Holiness meeting people in the village. It was a simple scene, no fuss. The people drew near to him with love in their eyes and he blessed them and conversed with them. His love for and deep interest in everyone was blissful to behold. After chatting to a long line of people, he inadvertently discovered J.P. behind a tree. He laughed and embraced our fine director with passion. It was the beginning of an important friendship.

As we flew away from Little Lhasa, I closed my eyes and hummed quietly, *"Om Mani Padme Hum"*.

Two weeks later I was flying in a single-engined Pilantus plane with David Breashears and J.P., taking aerial shots of Mount Everest for our film. It was haunting to see the gigantic terrain where we had been in the spring. It was dawn and the sun was breaking on the Goddess Mother of the Earth, or *Yankiamuntakim*, as the Dalai Lama called it. Far away, for as far as the eye could see, was distant Tibet, the pink glow of the sun lighting up the giant mountains of that country, one by one.

There was no wind from that ancient land of Bo. All was quiet and still. Who would have thought that an invasion had taken place there?

What of Wangdu? Where is he now? It is rumoured that years ago a Nepalese Army drove him out of Mustang after destroying his army. Wangdu fled with only forty men, over the mountainous terrain into Tibet itself. There he was hounded by Chinese and Nepalese troops. His exploits made the adventures of the Scarlet Pimpernel look like hide and seek.

It is said, though I cannot believe it is true, that on a high pass in August 1974, known as "Tinker", a massive ambush was laid for him. There, reminiscent of *Bonnie and Clyde*, he was riddled with bullets, and his bones lay bleached in the dry Tibetan air. But who knows? Will he not return? Will he not emerge at night from his hidden fortress in the heart of Lo, with his horsemen, on their swift, light-brown horses with blond manes and big black, bald-headed hunting dogs and terrorise the Chinese garrisons once more?

Who has the correct solution to the Chinese problem? I mused. Wangdu, with his war-like alarms and excursions, or the Dalai Lama with his smiling face and message of peace and love? Being an actor, my thoughts turned to the famous words of Shakespeare's Othello: "Keep up your bright swords, for the dew will rust them."

As our plane soared alongside the ramparts of Everest's West Ridge, my thoughts turned to China.

Modern Communist China gets a rough press these days. China's long history is crammed with achievements. Its people were writing poetry, spinning rare divine silks and dazzling the mind with art and philosophy when our civilisation was still in its infancy. Oh, it's all very complex and requires long thought. Whatever would Lao-Tzu and Confucius have made of it all? Maybe Confucius, on his death-bed, foresaw what would happen in China, when he said, whilst looking on the majestic dome of Tiai Shan, China's sacred mountain:

> "The Sacred mountain is falling.
> the beam is breaking,
> the wise man is withering away."

As we finished our filming of Everest from the Pilantus plane, my thoughts turned again to the Dalai Lama. When I met him, what impressed me most was his humour, gentleness and overwhelming belief in the good of mankind. He radiates hope. He believes that love and peace are the only way forward. He embraces all religions, echoing St Paul's words, "One spirit, many gifts."

The Dalai Lama's favourite verse is found in the writings of the renowned eighth-century Buddhist saint, Shantideva:

> "For as long as space endures
> and for as long as living beings remain,
> until then may I too abide
> to dispel the misery of the World."

CHAPTER
TWELVE

The Most Happy Fella

Well, ladies and gentlemen, here I am sitting in my study writing these last few words to bring to an end my third book. It has been a happy experience to share these adventures with you.

It is 6 a.m. on Sunday, 8 August 1993. The light outside is now increasing in brightness and soon it will be time to let my ducks out of their nocturnal quarters. Not quite yet though, for Ferdy the Fox is still about. Those of you who live in the country will know exactly what I mean. There is no animal to compare to the fox for cunning. A few weeks ago he had my old grey duck in his mouth and I raced up to him and roared, "How dare you? You swine! Put the bloody duck down." Amazingly he did so and, after giving me a sheepish look, cleared the fence and disappeared. The duck joined the others for a swim on the pond, came out, preened herself and gobbled all the soaked bread in sight, having forgotten that anything untoward had ever happened. Such is life.

We have scores of different farmyard ducks: white Aylesburies, Khaki Campbells, Muscovies, Black Cayugas, crossbreeds, raucous Call-Ducks, plus all manner of passing Mallards. The barn, stables, paddocks and garden are full of them. They are delightful company. We have hens too, strutting about, not to mention numerous ponies and dogs and cats and millions of moles. As we throw out the food in various places, the birds of the air eat us out of house and home. Still, we wouldn't have it any other way. Oh! I'm forgetting! I also have a 10,000-gallon pond stocked with a fine collection of multi-coloured Koi-Carp. I love my pond and find it a source of great relaxation.

All in all, we have about three acres of land with paddocks, lawns, shrubs and a tiny wood. Our "cottage" is just a simple bungalow, in truth, and sits just inside a beautiful large estate that the owner, the redoubtable Major Spowers, has formed into a trust. His tender care has shaped it into a paradise: small lakes whose banks flourish with all manner of flowers, giant rhubarb, azaleas, rhododendra, maple trees and Japanese acers. The waterways contain a multitude of pond life, including great crested and smooth newts, their smooth rhythm only slightly disturbed by the surface coots, and wild ducks. Trees are the Major's great love, and he calls it "The Arboretum". The variety and beauty of the trees is a wonder.

My wife and I are in our mid-fifties and looking after so many creatures is a full-time job, particularly when running a professional life as well. Most of the animals are rescued, quite a few come from the local RSPCA. We have always had generous help from kind young teenagers from nearby villages but, as our animal sanctuary has grown, it has become increasingly difficult to cope.

Therefore, much to our relief, a young man called Stephen Gittins has arrived in our life and has become my personal assistant. What a huge difference he has made to the property. I have known this fine man for several years, and my wife has known him since 1973 when she lived in Norfolk. He is our daughter Rosalind's godfather. About five feet ten inches tall, slim and handsome, he is a positive powerhouse of energy. Fleet of foot, he has eight ponies and one horse out into the fields in next to no time. Before you can say Jack Robinson, he also has the stables "mucked out" and the water buckets and hay nets filled. By mid-morning this is completed and he makes his way back and sits in his small study and, still perspiring, commences to tackle the complexities of my life.

This is far from easy as, in my upper middle age, I now seem to have three careers: acting, writing and exploration. At a time when I should be taking life more easily, I am actually increasing my work load! Until Stephen appeared on the scene I was finding it all quite a strain. The mail I receive is staggering. The garage was stacked up with it in black polythene bags and I had not a hope of answering it. I was beginning to let a lot of nice people down. The phone drove me up the wall, ringing every five minutes. This I found particularly exhausting. All this has been rectified by Stephen.

It is rare in this day and age to find someone with such sensitivity and integrity. So please don't ring him up and offer him a job! He is ours! Even if we have to chain him to the duck house! He is a realist, and when I enthuse about a goodly sum of money I am going to earn to help feed our menagerie, he always brings me down to earth by saying, "Yes, but don't forget, forty per cent goes to the Tax Man!" I give most of my friends different "Yeti" names and I therefore refer to Stephen as "The Forty Percent Yeti".

My wife is a tower of strength and organises all our days. God knows how she puts up with my bizarre behaviour and potty ideas. Without her common sense, practicality and vision I would be lost. Her devotion and care of all living things at Beeches Cottage is phenomenal.

My daughter too, eighteen now, and as pretty as a picture, fills the place with her warmth and personality. She will be going to University this autumn and I am immensely proud of her.

You can see, ladies and gentlemen, that I am a lucky man, "A most happy fella". Which, incidentally, is a musical by Frank Loesser, in which I played the title role of Tony for BBC Radio 2, at the Golders Green Hippodrome. It was a daunting experience, as the show was live. I don't read music and the part of Tony requires operatic singing of the highest quality. The cast consisted of top artists from the world of opera, and I was absolutely terrified! I spent many sleepless nights wondering how I would cope.

The conductor, the BBC concert orchestra and the cast were kindness itself and skilfully guided me through every crochet and quaver. But the whole enterprise would have been quite beyond me if it had not been for the brilliance of my music and singing teacher, Dorothy Kirkman. At one point I was on the verge of giving up.

It was at this moment that Hildegard held my hand and challenged me to go for it.

I have very little confidence. This image that Brian Blessed is a tough man with the courage of a lion is absolute rot! Whenever I am offered a part, my first reaction is that I cannot do it. After a while, I gain courage and convince myself that I can.

It is now 9.30 a.m. and I have been writing this chapter over the past three hours. The ducks and hens are outside my window and Stephen is giving the ponies their breakfast. In six hours' time I am going from Gatwick Airport to Kathmandu in Nepal to attempt to climb Mount Everest. Over the past few days I have alternated between quiet confidence and terrible uncertainty. I flatter myself that I am brave and strong, when really I often feel quite weak with a clear streak of yellow running down my back. I'll be all right — won't I? I've completed my training. I feel fit, I suppose. I have all my kit, although it is still spread out over my room. . . . Where's Stephen? I'll shout for him soon. Oh God, I'm scared, and I desperately miss my family already. . . . I'll phone Mum and Dad in a minute. There's no reason why a man of my age should not do well on Everest. Fifty-seven! I'll be the oldest man so far if I get up. Anyway that's not why I'm going. Sure I'm taking William, the Royal Marsden Bear, with me, along with the Frimley Park Hospital flag and the Dalai Lama's scarf, hopefully to place them on the summit. Summit, I ask you, I make it sound like Kinder Scout! But why am I going? I just don't know. I can quote you a million esoteric and philosophical reasons but it still doesn't make sense. It simply feels right. It feels a fine thing to do. I'm going for the hell of it.

I've been doing my one-man show all over the country and people, it seems, are fired up by the Everest theme. The year 1993 is forty years since it was first climbed. I have tried to impart to audiences that we all have our own Everests: "I'm going to ride that horse," or "I am going to complete my allotment and tell that uncle I've hated for thirty years that I love him." The hospitals are full of people conquering their own personal Everests. So why do we feel impoverished and imprisoned and in such need of adventure? Is it the fault of government?

Two days ago I went down to London to do some dubbing. A taxi driver took me to the studios in Dean Street. On the way, he suddenly stopped on Westminster Bridge, got out of the taxi and shouted with all his might at the members of Parliament, who were having morning coffee in the shade under the canopies alongside the House of Commons by the river: "You bastards! I hate you. You untalented creeps. If you had brains you'd be bloody dangerous! You should be bloody sacked. You're a poor lot . . . Guy Fawkes had the right bloody idea. I've a good mind to come and blow you all up myself. You bastards!"

All this was clearly heard by the shocked politicians. Still, in many ways the irate behaviour of the taxi driver epitomised the frustrations of a great many people today. Well, the world is certainly in the most frightful turmoil. When is it ever not?

I always keep in mind the image of Pandora. She opened the box and released all those furies. Then, when she realised what she had done, she attempted to close the lid and a little voice said, "Let me out! Let me out!" Pandora did so and a small creature flew out. Spreading her wet, iridescent wings in the morning light she said, "I am Hope, I am Hope."

Ladies and gentleman, we have hope!

I must pack and obey the siren call of the "Goddess Mother of the Earth". When I was a child my mother and father always used to sing to me in our back garden:

"You'll find happiness lies, right under your eyes,
back in your own back yard.
You may go to the East, go to the West, someday
        you'll find,
your weary heart back where you started from."

It also puts me in mind of T. S. Eliot's words: "We shall not cease from exploration and the end of all our exploring will be to arrive where we started and know it for the first time."

It remains for me to say once again: "Follow your dream. Go for it! And don't let the bastards grind you down."

LARGE PRINT

ISIS publish a wide range of books in large print, from fiction to biography. A full list of titles is available free of charge from the address below. Alternatively, contact your local library for details of their collection of ISIS books.

Details of ISIS unabridged audio books are also available.

Any suggestions for books you would like to see in large print or audio are always welcome.

ISIS
7 Centremead
Osney Mead
Oxford OX2 0ES
(0865) 250333

BIOGRAPHY AND AUTOBIOGRAPHY

David Bret	**Maurice Chevalier**
Sven Broman	**Garbo on Garbo**
Pauline Collins	**Letter to Louise**
Earl Conrad	**Errol Flynn**
Quentin Falk	**Anthony Hopkins**
Clive Fisher	**Noël Coward**
Sir John Gielgud	**Backward Glances**
Reggie Grenfell & Richard Garnett	
	Joyce By Herself and Her Friends (A)
Michael Hordern	**A World Elsewhere**
Joanna Lumley	**Stare Back and Smile**
Shirley MacLaine	**Dance While You Can**
Arthur Marshall	**Follow the Sun**
Sheriday Morley	**Robert, My Father**
Michael Munn	**Hollywood Rogues**
Peter O'Toole	**Loitering With Intent**
Adua Pavarotti	**Pavarotti**
Hilton Tims	**Once a Wicked Lady**
Peter Underwood	**Death in Hollywood**
Alexander Walker	**Elizabeth**
Aissa Wayne	**John Wayne, My Father**
Jane Ellen Wayne	**Clark Gable**
Jane Ellen Wayne	**The Life and Loves of Grace Kelly**

BIOGRAPHY AND AUTOBIOGRAPHY

Winifred Beechey	**The Reluctant Samaritan**
Christabel Bielenberg	**The Road Ahead**
Kitty Black	**Upper Circle**
Navin Chawla	**Mother Teresa**
Phil Drabble	**A Voice in the Wilderness**
Daphne du Maurier	**The Rebecca Notebook and Other Stories**
Lady Fortescue	**Perfume From Provence**
Gillian Gill	**Agatha Christie**
Paul Heiney	**Farming Times**
Paul Heiney	**Second Crop**
Brian Hoey	**The New Royal Court**
Ilse, Countess von Bredow	**Eels With Dill Sauce**

BIOGRAPHY AND AUTOBIOGRAPHY

Paul James	**Margaret**
Paul James	**Princess Alexandra**
John Kerr	**Queen Victoria's Scottish Diaries**
Margaret Lane	**The Tale of Beatrix Potter**
Bernard Levin	**The Way We Live Now**
Margaret Lewis	**Ngaio Marsh**
Vera Lynn	**Unsung Heroines**
Peter Medawar	**Memoir of a Thinking Radish**
Michael Nicholson	**Natasha's Story**
Angela Patmore	**Marje**
Marjorie Quarton	**Saturday's Child**
Martyn Shallcross	**The Private World of Daphne Du Maurier**
Frank and Joan Shaw	**We Remember the Blitz**
Joyce Storey	**Our Joyce**
Douglas Sutherland	**Born Yesterday**
James Whitaker	**Diana v. Charles**

(A) Large Print books also available in Audio

GENERAL NON-FICTION

Eric Delderfield	**Eric Delderfield's Bumper Book of True Animal Stories**
Caroline Elliot	**The BBC Book of Royal Memories 1947-1990**
Joan Grant	**The Cuckoo on the Kettle**
Joan Grant	**The Owl on the Teapot**
Helene Hanff	**Letters From New York**
Martin Lloyd-Elliott	**City Ablaze**
Elizabeth Longford	**Royal Throne**
Joanna Lumley	**Forces Sweethearts**
Vera Lynn	**We'll Meet Again**
Desmond Morris	**The Animal Contract**
Anne Scott-James and Osbert Lancaster	**The Pleasure Garden**
Les Stocker	**The Hedgehog and Friends**
Elisabeth Svendsen	**Down Among the Donkeys**
Gloria Wood and Paul Thompson	**The Nineties**
The Lady Wardington	**Superhints for Gardeners**
Nicholas Witchell	**The Loch Ness Story**

TRAVEL, ADVENTURE AND EXPLORATION

Jacques Cousteau	**The Silent World**
Peter Davies	**The Farms of Home**
Patrick Leigh Fermor	**Three Letters From the Andes**
Keath Fraser	**Worst Journeys**
John Hillaby	**Journey to the Gods**
Dervla Murphy	**The Ukimwi Road**
Freya Stark	**The Southern Gates of Arabia**
Tom Vernon	**Fat Man in Argentina**
A Wainwright	**Wainwright in the Limestone Dales**
Dylan Winter	**A Hack in the Borders**

(A) Large Print books also available in Audio